UN-
BEAT-
ABLE!

**THE HISTORIC SEASON
of the
1998 WORLD CHAMPION
NEW YORK YANKEES**

ATTENTION: ORGANIZATIONS AND CORPORATIONS

Most HarperPaperbacks are available at special quantity discounts for bulk purchases for sales promotions, premiums, or fund-raising. For information, please call or write:

Special Markets Department, HarperCollins Publishers Inc.
10 East 53rd Street, New York, N.Y. 10022-5299.
Telephone: (212) 207-7528 Fax: (212) 207-7222.

UN-BEAT-ABLE!

THE HISTORIC SEASON
of the
1998 WORLD CHAMPION
NEW YORK YANKEES

George King

HarperPaperbacks
A Division of HarperCollinsPublishers

For Marge and George King, Mom and Dad.

HarperPaperbacks
A Division of HarperCollins*Publishers*
10 East 53rd Street, New York, NY 10022-5299

If you purchased this book without a cover, you should be aware that this book is stolen property. It was reported as "unsold and destroyed" to the publisher, and neither the author nor the publisher has received any payment for this "stripped book."

Copyright © 1998 by George King. All rights reserved. No part of this book may be used or reproduced in any manner whatsoever without written permission except in the case of brief quotations embodied in critical articles and reviews. For information address HarperCollins Publishers Inc., 10 East 53rd Street, New York, NY 10022-5299.

ISBN 0-06-102014-1

HarperCollins®, ®, and HarperPaperbacks™ are trademarks of HarperCollins Publishers Inc.

Cover photograph © 1998 by Francis Specker/*New York Post*.

First printing: October 1998

Printed in the United States of America

Visit HarperPaperbacks on the World Wide Web at
http://www.harpercollins.com

98 99 00 ❖/OPM 10 9 8 7 6 5 4 3 2 1

Contents

The 1998 New York Yankees Team Records

1. With 114 wins, the Yankees finished second on the all-time, single-season win list:

116 – 1906 Chicago Cubs (36 losses)
114 – 1998 NY Yankees (48 losses)
111 – 1954 Cleveland Indians (43 losses)
110 – 1909 Pittsburgh Pirates (42 losses)
          1927 NY Yankees (44 losses)
109 – 1961 NY Yankees (53 losses)
          1969 Baltimore Orioles (53 losses)
108 – 1970 Baltimore Orioles (54 losses)
          1975 Cincinnati Reds (54 losses)
          1986 NY Mets (54 losses)

2. At 114–48, the Yankees established an American League record for **most wins in a single season,** breaking the mark of 111 by the 1954 Cleveland Indians.

3. Finished the season **66 games over .500,** equaling the franchise record set by the 1927 club (110–44). Prior to 1998, the last major league team to be as many as 66 games over .500 was the 1954 Cleveland Indians, who were 68 games over at 111–43.

4. At 114–48, established the major league record for **most wins in a 162 game schedule,** surpassing the 1961 Yankees and the 1969 Baltimore Orioles (both were 109–53).

5. Won 62 home games in 1998, equaling the second highest total in franchise history with the 1932 club (62–15). Only the 1961 club (65–16) won more games at home than the '98 Yankees.

6. Held lead in 48 consecutive games, a major league record. The streak started on June 28 in a 2–1 loss to the Mets at Shea Stadium and was snapped on August 20 in a 9–4 loss at Minnesota—the Yankees were 37–11 in those 48 games. The previous mark of 40 consecutive games with a lead was held by the 1932 Yankees.

7. Were 61–20 in their first 81 games, breaking the 162-game-schedule-record of the 1970 Cincinnati Reds (58–23). The major leagues went to the 162 game schedule in 1961.

8. Reached their **100th win on September 4,** breaking the major league record for the earliest calendar date to reach the century mark (previous record was held by the 1906 Cubs and 1954 Indians, who both won their 100th game on September 9).

9. The Yankees total of **207 home runs** was the second highest in franchise history, behind only the 1961 club's 240. Their 207 total was the highest in baseball history for a team without a single player with thirty or more home runs (surpassing the 1996 Detroit Tigers total of 204). The '98 Yankees were the forty-fourth team in Major League history to hit at least 200 home runs.

10. Finished **22 games ahead of the Boston Red Sox,** the widest margin of victory in franchise history (the previous high was 19 1/2 games over Detroit in 1936).

11. With **24 straight series without a loss,** the Yankees tied the major league record of the 1912 Boston Red Sox and the 1970 Cincinnati Reds, who also went 24 straight series without a loss within one season. The record streak began with a two-game split at Oakland (April 4–5) and ended with the Yankees losing two of three games at Baltimore (June 15–17). Prior to the series at Baltimore, the Yankees did not lose a series since they were swept in two games at Anaheim to open the season.

12. Tied the major league record of the 1991 Cincinnati Reds for the **most players in double figures in home runs and stolen bases,** with six: Brosius—19/11; Curtis—10/21; Jeter—19/30; Knoblauch—17/30; O'Neill—24/15; and Williams—26/15.

13. Had **eight players with fifteen or more home runs** in 1998 (Strawberry, Martinez, O'Neill, Williams, Knoblauch, Jeter, Posada, and Brosius), tying the major league record of the 1991 Texas Rangers. The Yankees also tied the major league record of ten players in double digits in home runs set earlier this season by the Baltimore Orioles.

14. Were the first team this century to play **.700 baseball** in four consecutive months of any single season. In the first five months of the '98 season, the Yankees went 17–6 in April (.739), 20–7 in May (.741), 19–7 in June (.731), and 20–7 in July (.741), before finishing the month of August 22–10 (.688).

15. Reached **100 wins in their 138th game,** breaking the American League record for the fewest amount of games to reach the century mark (previous record was

140 games by the 1954 Cleveland Indians). The 1906 Chicago Cubs hold the major league record for the fewest games to reach 100 victories (132 games).

16. **Reached 90 wins in their 120th game,** tying the major league record of the 1944 St. Louis Cardinals.

17. Became only the sixth team this century—and the first since 1909—**to win their 100th game of the season with fewer than 40 losses.** Only the 1906 Chicago Cubs (100–32), 1902 Pittsburgh Pirates (100–34), 1909 Pittsburgh Pirates (100–36), 1904 New York Giants (100–37), and 1907 Chicago Cubs (100–39) had accomplished the feat since 1900.

18. **Clinched their seventh American League Eastern Division Championship at Boston on September 9.** This was the fastest clinching by a Yankee team since divisional play began in 1969, and the second fastest in the majors since 1969 (the 1975 Reds were the only team to clinch earlier, on September 9). The clinching was also the Yankees' second fastest in club history (the 1941 Yankees clinched the American League on September 4).

Preface:
Great Expectations

We always search for beginnings because that's our nature. When does a couple know they're headed for the altar? Or the lawyer's office? More often than not there is a defining moment in everybody's life; some good and some not so good. Lives and careers are often shaped by one incident that leads to a break.

For the 1998 World Champion Yankees, it wasn't the final out of the World Series. It wasn't the parade up the Canyon of Heroes in late October. And it wasn't David Wells's perfect game on May 17.

To reach the point where the Yankees intoxicating success started to boil, you have to crawl back to October 6, 1997. There, on an unusually muggy fall night at Cleveland's Jacobs Field, the Yankees were eliminated by the underdog Indians in Game 5 of the best-of-five AL Division Series.

Sandy Alomar's home run off Mariano Rivera helped steal Game 4 for the Indians, who were four outs away from extinction. Andy Pettitte didn't pitch very well in Game 5, a 4–3 defeat that ended on a stress-free fly ball to left field by Bernie Williams with the potential tying run on second base in pinch-runner Scott Pose.

Looking at Paul O'Neill and Derek Jeter in the cup-strewn first base dugout, you knew defeat had cut deep into their competitive souls. Four outs away from advancing to the ALCS, and instead they were going home.

Inside the clubhouse, depression smothered a room that was supposed to reek of celebratory champagne and cigars. At one end, O'Neill was explaining how he thought his two-out double in the ninth was out of the park. Across the spacious room, Bernie Williams stared into space, wondering how he managed to hit .118 (2–for–17) against a team he had a career .297 average against.

In between O'Neill and Williams, George Steinbrenner worked the room. On his way down from the luxury suite where he'd watched the game, the Boss predicted his club would be in the World Series next year. No, he wasn't angry about being booted from the postseason by the Indians. Instead, his chest was out and he was calling O'Neill a "warrior."

"Nothing to be ashamed about," the Boss said as he shook limp hands in the quiet clubhouse. "We will be back."

Eventually, the sound of shower heads firing water at tired bodies was heard. Slowly, players gathered their gear and prepared to go home. Tomorrow they would be at Yankee Stadium to clear out their lockers instead of getting ready to play the Orioles in the ALCS.

Shortly afterward, the moment that would define the coming 1998 season occurred. On two runways at Cleveland's airport, developments were unfolding that would go a long way in returning the Yankees to the top of the baseball world.

On one of those runways, the Yankees charter carrying players, coaches, manager Joe Torre, and GM Bob Watson took off for Newark Airport, New Jersey. On another, Steinbrenner and the "Tampa Mafia" headed to Florida's West Coast.

"Devastated," was the way David Cone remembers the mood on the charter. "We expected to win the series. Not taking anything away from the Indians, but people were crushed. In the back of the plane, Bernie was a mess."

Always the team leader, Cone sensed something needed to be done to rally his teammates. On other teams Cone played for, several beverage carts full of beer, wine, and booze would have been emptied while a high-stakes poker game unfolded in the rear of the plane. But that wasn't going to happen with this bunch. Twenty-five altar boys they weren't, but they certainly weren't the type to find solace in the bottom of a glass.

No, Cone figured that nothing would happen on the plane, and that if anything were to happen at all, it would have to be after they touched down. So he dialed a friend who owned a bar on Fourteenth Street in Manhattan and told him that he had some spirits that needed lifting. The Yankees would be landing at Newark about 2:30 A.M., Cone said, and could his buddy keep the joint open?

Meanwhile, Steinbrenner's private jet was heading south. On board were Mark Newman, Gordon Blakeley, Billy Connors, and the Boss. The first three were Steinbrenner's trusted aids, a trio of workaholics who spend their days navigating the land mines that are hidden in every nook and cranny of the Yankees universe. Occasionally, you see their names in print. However, like

Mob capos, you rarely saw them in photos. John Gotti had his Ravenite Social Club on Mulberry Street; these guys have a state-of-the-art complex in Tampa where they work out of.

Newman, the head of a minor league system that ranks second to none in baseball, is a lawyer and a former head coach at Southern Illinois University. Blakeley, a former high school coach in Southern California and scout with Seattle, is the director of player personnel. Connors, a former Syracuse University point guard and well-respected major league pitching coach, is the organization's pitching guru.

Along with Gene Michael, the director of major league scouting, and Lin Garrett, the director of scouting, these three men are the power brokers in the organization, and are known throughout the game as the Boss's Baseball People.

If Connors, Newman, and Blakeley were counting on catching some sleep on the way home, the Boss had other ideas. Fired up, he immediately wanted to know what his club needed to do in order to improve.

The Boss had already made plans to boot disgruntled Charlie Hayes out of the Bronx. According to an exclusive story in the *New York Post* the day after the Yankees were eliminated from the playoffs, Hayes had played his last game. There was no way he was coming back. According to a team source, the Boss was ready to pay whatever team took Hayes the full $2 million he was owed.

What was significant in this think tank at 30,000 feet was that key ideas were being tossed around without any input from Watson. To an outsider, that seemed weird, since Watson was the GM. But to anybody with an idea about how things worked in Yankeeville, it was business as usual. Watson had become a fifth wheel. In fact, he called the *Post* in response to the Hayes story, wanting to know who the source had been, and in the course of discussion, Watson said he'd be surprised if the Yankees would swallow that much money on a player who possessed above-average skills.

"George heard stories about Hayes that he cringed at," a source said. "When Hayes's name kept surfacing in things, he made the decision to get rid of him."

Tommy Tanzer, Hayes's respected agent, was livid and called the *Post*. He said the paper didn't know what was going on, and he guaranteed that Hayes wouldn't be let go. The only thing wrong with Tanzer's rap was that he'd talked to Watson and not the Boss.

But concerning next year's Yankees, there were more problems than getting rid of Hayes. It was apparent that Cecil Fielder wasn't being brought back to be the designated hitter. And nobody in the organization wanted to see Derek Jeter hit leadoff again. So, third base, second base, and DH were hot topics in the air.

"They looked at me like I was crazy," the Boss said. "We started working before we took off and never stopped. We came up with a plan that was very important."

Since they'd come close to trading for Chili Davis during the season, it was generally assumed the veteran free agent DH would sign with the Yankees. The fact that Davis was represented by Tom Reich, a longtime confidant to Steinbrenner, only made it easier. Another name that surfaced was Chuck Knoblauch. Steinbrenner had long admired the pesky Twins leadoff hitter and brought his name up. Finally, somebody—and the Boss couldn't remember who it was—mentioned that Scott Brosius was going to be put on the block by the cash-strapped Oakland A's.

By the time the plane landed, the Yankees had a plan that would cost the Boss a significant amount of money and young players, and would improve the Bombers on three fronts.

Meanwhile, Cone had rounded up enough teammates to hang out. What he didn't know was that his friend had placed calls to various strip clubs, inviting dancers to stop by.

"The idea was to keep everybody together," Cone said. "A few of us knew it was a real bad time, and this team had been very close. We saw no harm in going down there and making sure everybody knew we were all in this together. We had no idea it would turn out the way it did."

And while somebody with a camera clicked away and then dropped the pictures off at the *Post*, which used them on the front page on October 8, the outing had served its purpose.

"That night was important because we needed each other," Cone said. "I think it set the tone for this year."

That night also made David Wells unhappy. Posing for pictures with the owner, Wells never in his wildest dreams thought he would wind up on the front page of the *New York Post* looking like death. Inside, there were pictures of Cone, Charlie Hayes, and Wells. The story painted an early morning picture of boobs and bats mixing it up over booze.

There was an outraged reaction. Many people couldn't understand how ballplayers could react to a crushing loss in that manner. What was supposed to be a rally of support for Bernie Williams, turned into a public relations nightmare.

"Here we tried to do something nice, and we wound up getting ripped for it," Cone said.

From there, the Yankees went about implementing the plan hatched on the plane.

Kenny Rogers, as nice a guy as there is in baseball, had been the latest player to be accused of not being able to handle New York. There had also been some questions about the health of his left shoulder throughout his two-year stay in pinstripes. And while Joe Torre genuinely liked Rogers as a person, he didn't always appreciate him not telling the entire truth when asked how healthy he was.

So when the A's made it very clear that Brosius was not being brought back, the Yankees shipped Rogers to Oakland on November 7 for the smooth-fielding third baseman who had gone from hitting .304 in 1996 to .203 in 1997. For the Yankees, the deal served two purposes: (1) they were getting rid of Rogers—even if they had to pay $5 million of the $10 million left on his contract, and (2) Brosius would give them far better defense at third than they'd had with Boggs and Hayes. And maybe he could hit .250.

Four days later Hayes was gone, also shipped to the Bay area. While Hayes has a reputation as a malcontent, a player who wears out his welcome at every stop, he has an uncanny way of returning to teams. He was going to the Giants for minor league outfielder Chris Singleton, and it would be his second stint with the club he broke into the majors with in 1988. Since then Hayes had two tours of duty with the Phillies and the Yankees, in addition to one stop with the Rockies and Pirates.

A month later, $9.8 million of Steinbrenner's money was used to land Chili Davis. Instantly, the Yankees had a force from both sides of the plate to plug a hole that Fielder couldn't, due to declining bat speed and a thumb injury.

On February 3, Bob Watson decided he'd had enough of Steinbrenner. Under the mistaken impression when he left the GM's job in Houston after the 1995 season that the GM of the Yankees would run the Yankees, Watson was frustrated at the layers that one had to peel back in order to get things done. Rising blood pressure gave him a scare in May of 1997. The Boss understood, told Watson to cut back on the seventy-hour work weeks, and agreed that Watson needed time to exercise daily.

Still, Watson was tired of the Boss. And he wasn't in the best of standings with the Tampa family, either. Not after telling a gathering of people in January that Steinbrenner's Baseball People were "little voices that ran around in his head."

Not knowing that quote would work its way into the newspapers, Watson was furious when it did. But not as mad as the Tampa office was. Relations between the Bronx and Tampa, never on a level that could be considered good, were now very low. Newman, Blakeley, Connors, and Garrett worked long hours for the demanding Boss. Along the way they had built the Yankees farm system into a talent-producing machine. To have Watson belittle them, they felt, was wrong.

So, on February 3, Watson stepped aside with an agreement that Steinbrenner would pay him the remainder of the $400,000 he was owed.

"It's not like I sneak up on people," the Boss said.

"They know what it's like when they come to work for me."

In Brian Cashman, the Boss had an assistant GM who had worked for the Yankees for ten years. Starting as a minor league intern in 1986, Cashman only knew one way to operate, and that was in the often chaotic world of the Yankees. When the Boss asked the then–thirty-year-old assistant if he wanted to follow Watson, Cashman said yes and agreed to a one-year deal.

Two days later the trade for Knoblauch, which was totally brokered by Steinbrenner, Twins GM Terry Ryan, and Knoblauch's agents—Alan and Randy Hendricks—was finalized. Knoblauch wasn't cheap. He'd make $6 million a year for the next four seasons, and he cost the Yankees left-handed pitcher Eric Milton, their top pitching prospect, in addition to shortstop prospect Cristian Guzman.

Now, a week before leaving for spring training, the Boss had his team intact. That meeting in the sky had led to a plan, and he'd carried it out. As for the battered psyche of his players, Cone was pretty sure the abbreviated Boys Night Out had served its purpose.

Now, the Bombers were ready for a return trip to the top of the baseball world.

Part 1

Chasing History:
The 1998 Season

1

Cameramen, Divas, and Spring Training

Through sunglasses, Joe Torre watched a Legends Field infield drill that first day of spring training in late February 1998. He looked at second base and saw Chuck Knoblauch where a year ago he had a disgruntled Mariano Duncan still stewing about not getting a multiyear deal, and an often-confused Pat Kelly who was the regular second baseman one minute and a pinch-runner the next. It didn't help that neither one hit enough to please and their defense was below average.

Now he had Knoblauch, a free agent hired away from the Minnesota Twins, a legitimate leadoff hitter who would enable Torre to bat Derek Jeter second. And Knoblauch was coming off a Gold Glove year, a four-time All-Star who had to be better than Duncan and Kelly.

At third base was Scott Brosius, acquired from the Oakland A's in a trade for the underachieving pitcher Kenny Rogers. Torre had no idea if Brosius could hit enough to warrant playing a corner position on a team that was expected to win it all for the second time in three seasons. After all, he had a brutal 1997 in which he batted .203, a departure from his career average of .267. Still, he was a solid fielder and would more than make up for the departures of Wade Boggs, whose hunt for 3,000 hits landed him in Tampa playing for something called the Devil Rays, and Charlie Hayes, whose Me-First reputation was in San Francisco, where he would be Giants manager Dusty Baker's starter.

Of course, first base and shortstop were rock-solid, with Tino Martinez and Derek Jeter performing beyond expectations. Behind the plate, Joe Girardi was back and the youngster Jorge Posada was worth further consideration. In the outfield, Bernie Williams and Paul O'Neill had center field and right field locked up. Left field was more of an open question, but it was a happy dilemma to be choosing between Darryl Strawberry, Tim Raines, and Chad Curtis.

Offensively, Torre knew the lineup that added Chili Davis certainly had enough muscle, even if Brosius had a mediocre year. What other A.L. team could send up to the plate a lineup that included Knoblauch, Jeter, Paul O'Neill, Bernie Williams, Tino Martinez, and Davis?

So, defensively and offensively, things looked decent. But did Torre have enough arms?

"Everything we do is based on pitching, and that is the biggest question mark for us, absolutely," Torre said.

Dwight Gooden had gone to Cleveland after trashing Torre on the way out of the Bronx, and Kenny Rogers was in Oakland. Torre was left with David Wells, David Cone, Hideki Irabu, Andy Pettitte, and Ramiro Mendoza.

Yes, Wells was coming off a career-high sixteen wins, and pitched a wonderful game against the Indians in the playoffs. But could he be counted on to be the staff ace? Would that negative body language Torre talked about so much in 1997 surface too many times for the manager's liking? Could Wells stay focused for six long, grueling months?

When Wells reported to camp eight pounds over the desired 240 pounds, Torre mentioned it and then let it go. No sense getting into a pissing match with a guy he knew he was going to need. And besides, Wells had arrived heavier to his first camp a year earlier and admitted to beating the Indians in the A.L. Division Series while pitching at 250 pounds.

Then there was David Cone, who at thirty-five was coming off shoulder surgery. Would his arm hold up? Would he be as effective? And Pettitte had done a wonderful job of hiding back spasms across the second half of 1997, but there was no guarantee he could avoid them again. And Ramiro Mendoza had just 26 major league starts on his résumé. Could he last a season?

The key to the picture seemed to be Hideki Irabu. A $12.8 million bust in 1997, Irabu was no longer an international marketing cash cow for George Steinbrenner's trophy shelf. It was time for Irabu to step up.

"I think it will be different for him because his attitude and approach will have to change," Torre said of Irabu, who was 5–4 with an obese 7.09 ERA in 13 games (nine starts), and a lightning rod for criticism due to a surly attitude and minimal work ethic in 1997. "Last year he was dropped out of the sky and into the middle of a season that was not easy to handle. Spring training will tell us, but he will definitely have the opportunity to win a starting job.

"Shape and weight go hand in hand, but if you go

through spring training," Torre explained, "you may be able to carry some extra weight and get away with it. But if you are not in shape and have the extra weight, it's impossible. I have heard reports of twenty pounds, but we'll wait until he gets on the scale."

In his first spring outing on March 10 in Winter Haven against the hated Indians, Irabu showed his disgust with the umpire's strike zone and appeared to give up when things didn't go his way early. Furthermore, he got involved in a beanball war that ultimately resulted in Luis Sojo having his wrist broken by Jaret Wright.

Afterward, Joe Girardi criticized Irabu for acting in the same immature manner he had a year ago. Three days later the Yankees didn't know what to think in regard to their huge investment when he got into a confrontation with a Japanese television crew.

The outburst followed Irabu's strongest outing of the spring, when he shut out the Tigers across four innings. In discussing the effort with American media, Irabu was jovial. Later he was anything but.

Irabu believed he was having an off-the-record conversation with Japanese writers whom he believed had been far too critical and were invading his privacy. Kei-ichiro Hoashi, with Tokyo Sports Broadcast, turned his camera on. Irabu told him to turn it off and Hoashi fired back at Irabu, who then put his hands on the $60,000 camera.

"He kicked me foot-to-foot and tried to pull the camera from me," a distraught Hoashi said. "I was afraid he was going to crash my camera so I gave him the tape."

Irabu threw the tape to the cement floor and stomped on it several times before picking it up and placing it in his pocket. And he told still photographers that if they printed pictures of the melee, he would sue them. He then ordered the film removed from the cameras, ripped the film out of the canisters and threw it away.

Afterward, he stormed out to the parking lot and raced away.

"I think he is dangerous," said Hoashi, who didn't press charges against Irabu.

So much for the new and improved Irabu attitude.

Joe Torre, who was pleased with Irabu's work on the mound, refused to get into his boorish behavior. "I am not interested in that so we will clip that right here," Torre said. "You can deal with that with one of the gossip writers."

Ah, the gossip writers. They had descended upon Tampa after pop diva Mariah Carey surfaced at Legends Field to watch Derek Jeter. After a night game, Carey and Jeter strolled into the Tampa evening and ridiculous rumors begin to fly from coast to coast.

The most absurd was that Jeter and Carey had spent days together, never leaving his Tampa home. However, Jeter didn't miss so much as a minute of work. Therefore there had to be two Jeters—which, by the way, still wouldn't be enough for the ocean of female fans who adore him.

To Jeter, seeing his name connected to a superstar such as Mariah Carey was an eye-opener simply because he wasn't prepared for the reaction. Compared to the questions dealing with his contract—which had been going on for two springs—the questions about Carey and his personal life were difficult for him.

"I'll talk about baseball, but that's it," Jeter said, drawing a line that he intended to hold strongly. "They can write what they want but I am just talking about baseball."

Even teammates learned to stay away from clubhouse joking on the issue when Jeter didn't take kindly to some light razzing before a March 6 game in Clearwater against the Phillies. According to a Jack Russell Stadium clubhouse attendant, Jeter put an end to the joking quickly with stern words that shocked his teammates.

The situation reached its zenith a week later when Jeter was asked about a report that claimed he was prepared to give Carey an engagement ring.

"They have me getting engaged, that's great," Jeter said in a disgusted voice. "I am not getting engaged. Not today, not tomorrow. I am not getting married. Don't be afraid to write that, I am not getting married."

In the meantime, things ran as smoothly as they possibly could. Irabu apologized to Cashman, Torre, and the Yankees for his behavior, then proceeded to blow away the Braves on March 12 in Orlando, retiring all twelve batters he faced and fanning seven.

The gem came on the same day a *New York Post* story hinted that Irabu's right elbow wasn't a hundred percent. The story irked Torre, but eight days later Irabu was forced to cut short a bullpen workout. The next day while the Yankees were bombing the Royals at Legends Field, Irabu was at a nearby hospital undergoing X rays, a CAT scan, and an MRI. The tests disclosed tendinitis and a small bone spur in the elbow.

"From now on I will check with the *Post* to find out what's going on," said Torre, who is paid by the *Daily News* for doing promotional ads.

Meanwhile, Cuban defector Orlando "El Duque" Hernandez arrived on March 20 and immediately impressed with his outgoing attitude. One day after jumping into pinstripes, Hernandez wowed a large crowd that gathered on the walkways above a Legends Field bullpen in a thirteen-minute workout. Of course, nobody knew at that time what the Yankees were getting for the $6.6 million, but for the moment it appeared they weren't going to be in for the headaches that Irabu presented a year earlier.

Aside from Irabu, everything else clicked. The Boss said there was nothing to a story that had him talking to Cablevision about selling the Yankees. Cone's shoulder held up, Wells rounded into shape, Mendoza overcame a shoulder problem, Bernie Williams never once mentioned his contract situation, just as he'd promised the day he arrived after settling an arbitration case at $8.25 million. And Pettitte, who signed a $3.75 million deal and avoided arbitration, was Pettitte, which means he was self-critical and never satisfied.

That's why so many heads were turned by what he said on March 26, one day before the final exhibition game in Florida:

"I hate to say it, it all depends. You have to have so many things go right for you. You may have a stretch where somebody goes down or something and that may change the look of the lineup. But right now it is sickening how good we look."

The next day the Yankees traveled to Lakeland to play the Tigers, but all eyes were on Irabu, since he threw in the bullpen and didn't feel any discomfort in the elbow. Before leaving Florida, Torre said he would split left field between Darryl Strawberry and Chad Curtis and use Tim Raines off the bench. Within a week, when switch-hitting DH Chili Davis needed surgery to repair a tendon in his right ankle, those plans would change.

"Who knows, you don't play the damn thing on paper, unfortunately, because if we did we would have a pretty good shot at this thing," Torre said when asked how good his All-Star-dominated club could be. "It's the best lineup I have ever written down. The pitching isn't as deep as it has been the last couple of years, but if we can keep them healthy, we can hold our own."

After flying from Tampa to Tijuana because they had borrowed a luxury plane that couldn't land in San Diego, the Yankees survived a wild bus ride in which the driver ran the bus up a Mexican highway divider and nearly put the vehicle on its side. An ominous beginning to what would become a grim West Coast trip.

Instead of finding bright sunshine to work out in during a three-day stay in San Diego to play the Padres in the last of the exhibition games, the Yankees battled rain. On Saturday night David Wells, perhaps too jazzed up because he was pitching in the stadium he used to sneak into as a kid growing up on the salty streets of Ocean Beach, was knocked around and did not impress in his final tune-up. Sunday was rained out, a rarity in Southern California.

Monday was one of those days players quietly despise, since they were slated to play an exhibition game against San Diego State on the Aztecs field, which had been soaked by three days of rain. Another oddity: Wasn't this Southern California? It almost never rained here. However, it was the time of El Niño, and the weather system affecting the rest of the country in other ways was wreaking wet havoc on the Pacific Coast.

Because these were the Yankees, Dan Cunningham, the head groundskeeper at Yankee Stadium, was imported from the Bronx to make sure the field was playable. He spent all day Sunday working on the main mound as well as the bullpen mound. Still, All-Star closer Mariano Rivera tweaked a groin working the final inning. It remained to be seen how it would affect him in the days ahead.

Over the course of spring training, the buzz about the Yankees had built—a team of All-Stars, veterans who knew how to win, a potent lineup, solid defense and capable pitching. Could they win it all? All the hype only enlarged the bull's-eye that is constantly attached to the Yankees pinstriped backs.

"There is no doubt that teams will be gunning for the Yankees," Cone said. "Teams generally get up for the Yankees, but probably more so this year."

Finally, after watching the most talented team he had ever managed work its way into shape, Torre had a sobering message to Steinbrenner's $72 million collection of superstars:

"You remind yourself that just because you're supposed to win, that doesn't mean you're going to."

2

Men Without Bats

Joe Torre sat on an equipment trunk inside the visiting clubhouse at San Diego's Qualcomm Stadium. Six days away from Opening Day, he knew the heat was being turned up.

"George asked me the other day if any team went 162–0," Torre said.

Of course, Steinbrenner wasn't serious. But around him, you never know. After investing $72 million to put this team together, he spent March and April saying nothing more than "We will be in the mix."

However, everybody knew that if the Yankees were simply "in the mix," more than one person would be in trouble.

After the exhibition games against San Diego, the Yankees bused to Anaheim, reaching their hotel in the middle of Disney in time to rent a meeting room where they watched Kentucky defeat Utah for the NCAA basketball title. An indication of how close this bunch would be was found in the attendance: every player and coach—along with Torre—attended the function.

Tuesday brought a light workout, and Wednesday

delivered Andy Pettitte, in his first Opening Day assignment, against Yankee killer Chuck Finley.

"We are tired of talking about it," said Pettitte, an Opening Day starter for the first time in his career. "Now it's time to go out and play and we have to prove it. We start the mission we are on."

At 8:31 P.M., Pacific Coast Time, Finley threw the first pitch of the season to Chuck Knoblauch. Two hours and 52 minutes later, Finley had defeated Pettitte, 4–1, in the official opening of Edison Field, known as Anaheim Stadium before a $145 million renovation project came within a hideous-looking rock formation in center field of making it a baseball palace.

Afterward, there was no wringing of hands. Pettitte had given up four runs and nine hits in six innings, but Finley was Finley, and that meant he had his nasty split-fingered fastball working. No big deal, there were 161 games left.

Wrong. To the Boss in Tampa, losing on the same day the Devil Rays won the first game in their history pushed a button. When the Boss picked up the *Tampa Tribune* on April 2, he didn't care that Boston and Toronto were tied for first place in the A.L. East at 1–0. Or that the hated Orioles were 1–1. All he had eyes for was the expansion Devil Rays sporting a 1–1 mark, which put them one-half game ahead of the Yankees in the A.L. East race.

So the Boss did what he had done for twenty-five years since buying the Yankees: he roared.

"They better stop reading their press clippings," Steinbrenner warned. "They are behind Tampa Bay."

Suddenly, nothing else mattered. The Yankees were

behind the Devil Rays. When the Boss saw his words in print the next day, he was embarrassed. So much so that he spent the next days not returning phone calls from the media.

"He has told me that I'm running the team and that I should be the one talking," rookie GM Brian Cashman said.

So what happens the next night? The best lineup money could buy was limited to two runs by four pitchers, and the Angels belted Wells on their way to a 10–2 victory. In two games the high-priced batting order had produced three runs and was 1–for–16 with runners in scoring position.

Perhaps Yankee fans were getting nervous too. In the wee hours of Friday morning in the Anaheim Hilton, a huge Yankee fan in from Las Vegas announced that all the winter and spring training hype was a crock. That Wells was out of shape, Chili Davis wasn't worth the money, and Tim Raines moved like he was running uphill. When he got back to Vegas, Thomas King (the author's brother) said he was going to get even with the team he lives and dies with: he was going to bet against them.

"I am sitting right behind the dish tonight, closer to the plate than the mound is to the plate, and Wells had nothing," Tom King announced to nobody. "I mean nothing. The whole bunch of them had nothing. This team is in trouble. Big trouble."

I didn't have the heart to ask how much Wells & Co. had cost him back in Vegas.

True to his word, the Boss remained muzzled. However, he was stirring.

More rain washed out Friday night's action in Oakland. And when Scott Spiezio took David Cone deep for a grand slam in the five-run sixth, the A's were on their way to a 7–3 victory and the Yankees had dropped the first three of the season.

Incredibly, Torre's job security had become Issue No. 1 in the Yankee universe. Maybe not inside the clubhouse, but outside the door it was all panicked Yankee fans talked about. Would Torre last the trip? Davey Johnson, a Steinbrenner favorite from the mid-eighties, when his renegade Mets knocked the Boss off the back page of the *Post* nightly, was in Orlando, not working.

"Someday we will look back on this and laugh," Cashman predicted through a stiff upper lip.

Late Saturday afternoon, with his team 0–3 and now a full game behind Tampa Bay, Torre sat in his office and listened to job-related questions from *Post* baseball columnist Joel Sherman.

"I can't start worrying about that or I'll manage scared and distracted, and I can't do that," Torre said.

Meanwhile, Cone had been rocked for seven runs and seven hits in 5 1/3 innings by the Triple A's. And that muscle-bound lineup? In three games it had scored six runs and was 4–for–28 with runners in scoring position.

Surely the nightmare would end Sunday, right? And it did, but the Yankees needed two runs in the tenth, delivered on a sacrifice fly by Knoblauch and a Derek Jeter single to pull out a 9–7 victory over the putrid A's. Yet, the black cloud that followed the Yankees from San Diego to the Bay area was still lurking as Rivera had to leave the game in the ninth when the right groin injury was affecting his leg kick.

Add that to Chili Davis not having played since the second game due to a right ankle problem, and even the first victory of the year couldn't be celebrated.

Four games in, the Yankees were 1–3, their closer was hurt, and the switch-hitting DH Steinbrenner had paid $9.8 million for was on the shelf. Back in New York, Yankee fans were in a full-blown panic.

If it's true that you can't start to make your way back up until you hit rock bottom, the Yankees were wearing deep abrasions on April 6 in Seattle. After not seeing Randy Johnson, who had not yet quit on the Mariners, in 1997, the Yankees were going to miss the Big Unit in a three-game series inside the depressing Kingdome, a house of horrors for the Bombers in recent years.

Without Johnson, the Mariners were slated to start control freak Jamie Moyer, the slop-throwing Jim Bullinger, and soon-to-be journeyman Ken Cloude.

Surely, the lineup would build on the nine-run effort in Oakland the day before. And with Pettitte coming off a loss, there was an air of confidence in the clubhouse prior to the game. Even with Rivera being placed on the fifteen-day disabled list, gloom and doom hadn't descended on the Yankees.

Three hours later that same room was engulfed in depression as Men Without Bats picked at the postgame spread. The only sound to be heard was that of plastic knives moving food that really didn't want to be eaten around paper plates.

Thanks to Moyer's tantalizing change-up, Pettitte not being overly sharp, and Mike Buddie getting rocked in his major league debut, the Mariners were able to defeat the toothless Bombers, 8–0, in front of 27,445.

It was the Yankees fourth loss in five games, and very alarming because of the way the supposedly best lineup in baseball was manhandled again. Held to three window-dressing hits and striking out fifteen times, the Yankees were 0–for–7 with runners in scoring position. For the season they were hitting an anemic .171 (7–for–41) in the clutch.

"We can't score runs, there are no excuses, we just didn't play well," said No. 5 hitter Tino Martinez, who was 0–for–4, fanned three times, and combined with Paul O'Neill and Bernie Williams to go 0–for–11 and whiff nine times.

In addition, Lou Piniella's practice of telling his pitchers to back O'Neill off the plate continued when Moyer, who as one Yankee said, "Can throw a ball in a teacup, that's how good his control is," hit O'Neill in the third.

When Piniella managed O'Neill in Cincinnati, Sweet Lou wanted O'Neill to alter a punishing swing in order to hit homers. When O'Neill didn't buy into the theory, Piniella fumed. Ever since taking over the Mariners, Piniella's pitchers had pitched to O'Neill as if the area between the inside corner and O'Neill's navel was theirs.

"What they do to Paulie is a joke, a f——g joke," a Yankee uniform said.

What had transpired on the field was no joke. Not to the players, coaches, or Torre.

More often than not, Torre spends the postgame hours with friends. Having played forever and managed almost as long, Torre has an army of acquaintances in each city the Yankees visit. Rarely does a night go by on the road when his office doesn't have somebody dropping by to chat. Often, Torre winds up in a restaurant with friends or his coaches for a late night meal.

Not this night. Drained from watching Moyer stick it to his club, Torre headed for the Metropolitan Grill, requested a table in the back, and dined alone.

"Joe was pretty hard on himself," close friend Reggie Jackson said the next morning.

Prior to batting practice the next day, Torre swept the media out of the room and gathered his shocked team into the middle of it. Since it's not his style, Torre didn't go into a Knute Rockne rap. Instead he informed his players that he thought the Mariners may have intimidated them the night before. He also reminded them to stay aggressive. David Cone spoke along the same lines.

Of course, the specter of Steinbrenner loomed. He was in New York giving Yankee Stadium the white glove treatment in preparation for the home opener in four days.

"I really haven't had a whole lot of contact with George the three years I've been here," Torre said. "Obviously, we see each other when we're in New York. I would say over the two-plus years I have been here, I've called him more than he's called me."

Asked to describe his club's psyche, Torre admitted there were some lips scraping the clubhouse carpet.

"We're down and we're going to have to fight our way out of this thing," Torre said. "I don't care how good a club you are, you still are going to go through times when you have to find a way to turn it around."

Knoblauch started the climb off the canvas by hitting Bullinger's first pitch into the left-field seats to ignite a six-run first inning that included a two-run laser home run to center by Darryl Strawberry and a solo blast from Jorge Posada. All the juice was needed because Wells was gone before getting an out in the seventh. In between, Strawberry belted another two-run homer to center.

Still, Torre couldn't relax. With Rivera shelved, Torre called Mike Stanton into a bases-loaded, one out spot in the eighth with the Yankees on top, 11–7. Stanton responded by striking out Rick Wilkins and getting Tomas Perez on a stress-free foul pop to O'Neill. Stanton worked the final inning perfectly.

It was just the Yankees fifth win in the last 23 games at the Kingdome.

The pressure to leave the West Coast 3–4 or 2–5 was placed on Irabu's ample shoulders. Since he was facing the team that put him on the road to ruin in 1997, and because he hadn't been all that impressive against San Diego State, there weren't many who were confident the Yankees would be going home one game under the break-even point.

Yet, Irabu was more than effective. Even if he had command of just one pitch—a 95 mph fastball—Irabu was able to hold the Mariners to one run and four hits in five innings as the Yankees eked out a 4–3 victory. But the pitching star of the day was Stanton.

On the list of daunting baseball tasks, getting Ken Griffey, Jr. out in the bottom of the ninth inning with the tying run on third and the winning run on second and no outs, ranks at the top.

After giving up a leadoff homer to Russ Davis and consecutive singles to Joey Cora and Alex Rodriguez in the ninth, Stanton stared at baseball's best hitter as the crowd peeled the gray paint off the Kingdome with its lungs.

With the count full, Stanton decided not to play games with Griffey. If Griffey was going to starch him, he'd have to do it against his best pitch.

"In that situation, he's a fastball hitter and I'm a fastball pitcher," Stanton said. "I am not going away from my strength because it's his strength. It's time to party."

Stanton fed Griffey a middle-in fastball a little up, and Griffey skied to left. One pitch later, Stanton induced Edgar Martinez to hit into a game-ending double play that was saved by a jazzy scoop by Tino Martinez on Knob-lauch's throw from second.

With a pulsating 4–3 victory, the Yankees Road Trip from Hell didn't have as much sting in it. Two straight wins in the Kingdome, a House of Horrors for the Yan-kees, sent the Bombers home 3–4 and looking forward to the home opener against the hapless A's at Yankee Stadium.

"When you start a road trip and you're asked how about 3–4, you say no," Torre said. "But when you go 0–3 to start, 3–4 is pretty good."

Especially if you are embarrassed 8–0 in the first game and lose DH Chili Davis to the disabled list, only to bounce back and win the final two. In taking two of the three, the Yankees won a series at the Kingdome for the first time since 1994.

As they winged home, they knew they'd dodged a major bullet. A 3–4 record wasn't what they had in mind when they left Florida, but they would take it. And laugh about it by the end of the month.

Yankee Profile:
Derek Jeter

The first impression that seeps into the envious male mind is that it must be easy being Derek Jeter. No, make that very easy. While he hasn't reached millionaire status from baseball earnings yet, he will soon have more money than he knows what to do with. Blessed with movie star looks, a body *GQ* can't get enough of, and a level-headed outlook on life, Jeter is New York's most eligible bachelor. He plays shortstop for the Yankees and does it well enough that he will receive serious consideration for the American League MVP come November.

Yet, the easiest part of being Derek Jeter arrives at 7:35 every night. That is the start of a three-hour period when it's Jeter on a baseball field inhaling ground balls, going into the hole for others, and spraying line drives to all fields. On the field, Jeter is left alone by everybody else. He comes to us through television and can't be touched by an adoring fan base, bothered by questions about his social life, or have his privacy violated by autograph-seeking kooks. And he doesn't have to live in a hotel with his phone off the hook to keep female fans away from his door.

Yes, it would be fun to be Derek Jeter. For about a week or two. After that, the hassles he has to deal with would make the strongest man buckle.

He has been a Yankee for three seasons and can only shake his head at the rumors he hears about himself. It's said he was born in a hospital in Pequannock, New Jersey. Residents of that sleepy township twenty-six miles west of Manhattan tell each other that Jeter is buying a house near the Morris County golf course. Jeter is also rumored to be moving into Wayne, another New York bedroom community, east of Pequannock.

"Where does this stuff start?" Jeter, a native of Michigan, wants to know. "I mean I hear my name in so many things. I don't have a clue. I have never even heard of Wayne, New Jersey."

For the record, Jeter rents an apartment on Manhattan's Upper East Side and owns a modest home in Tampa. And that's it.

Away from both, he's almost become a prisoner of his budding fame. Not quite a hermit, Jeter is rarely, if ever, seen on the grounds of the hotels the Yankees stay in. Once, in the past two seasons, I've seen him at the team hotel. That was this past year in Texas, when he was lounging poolside. Other than that, he's been invisible.

However, that doesn't mean people don't try to get to him. And they'll stop at nothing.

One night late in the season, the Yankees were staying at the Renaissance Vinoy Resort in St. Petersburg. The hotel bar was less than half full when a young woman walked in and announced she was looking for Jeter. She introduced herself to various customers she believed were part of the Yankees traveling party. To one, she was Mary. To another, she was Cheryl. She told a third person her name was Patty.

She was dreaming. She had no chance of getting to Jeter's room on that night, the next night, or any night between then and eternity. Even after she stated, "I'll take care of you if you help me find him."

She went home disappointed because nobody believed her, and those who knew Jeter wouldn't betray his confidence. On the surface, it's no big deal to Jeter, because he wasn't downstairs getting hassled. But who knows what happens the next time? Maybe the next girl is a little more seductive, a bit more persuasive. Then what happens?

When it's not starstruck females attempting to get into his hotel room, it's an autograph-seeking geek, like the one who apparently bribed the woman delivering room service to Jeter's room at the Marriott in Baltimore's Inner Harbor.

"It was unbelievable," Jeter said. "I ordered something to eat, and right behind the person who delivered it was this guy. He came right in and asked me for my autograph."

Talk about chutzpah!

All the while, Jeter has kept most of his personal life a secret. There was the much-publicized brief fling with Mariah Carey, but otherwise, even some of his teammates don't know much about Jeter's life away from the ballpark. He answers every reporter's baseball questions, even the dumbest ones, of which there are many. There are times when he's terse, and other times when he's expansive. In that category, he's like a lot of other players. But his eyes go cold when somebody brings up his off-the-field life. Instantly, a shield comes over his face and the twinkle in his eye vanishes. No words are needed; you know you have gone to an area where you don't belong.

Meanwhile, New York's gossip pages can't get enough of Jeter. They have him in places he isn't. The kicker was a supposed three-day lovefest with Carey in his Tampa house in which they locked the doors and never came out. Interestingly, Jeter never missed a day of work during spring training, but the gossipers didn't bother checking that.

The dribs and drabs of talk you get from teammates is that Jeter never wants to be the center of attention when they go out in a group. Often he sits off to the side and blends into the scene as well as a budding superstar with Hollywood looks can. That his closest friend on the team is catcher Jorge Posada, a former minor league teammate who shares the Yankee catch-

ing duties with Joe Girardi, perhaps tells you better than anything else what kind of person Jeter is. So many times you see
the star leave the minor league teammate when they get to the
majors. Derek Jeter, it's nice to say, isn't like that.

On the diamond, Jeter has improved every year he has
played. A first-round pick of the Yankees in 1992—he was
the sixth pick overall—Jeter raced through the system. Today,
Yankee talent evaluators use him as the measuring stick for
good prospects. Drew Henson, currently a freshman quarterback at Michigan, was taken in the third round of this past
year's draft. Afraid he wouldn't sign a baseball contract, other
teams were scared off. Not the Yankees. They signed Henson
and he played ten games for the Tampa team in the Gulf
Coast League.

Asked to describe what Henson, a third baseman, looked
like, minor league head Mark Newman said, "He is a Jeter-
type player, he could make quick jumps up the ladder if he
stayed with baseball."

In the Yankees world there are no higher words of praise.

Of course, the question is how long Jeter will be a Yankee.
At first blush, it appears ridiculous that the Yankees wouldn't
want to lock him up with a long-term deal. Even after Boston
did that with shortstop Nomar Garciaparra and Philadelphia
did it with third baseman Scott Rolen—the A.L. and N.L.
Rookies of the Year in 1997, respectively—the Yankees paid
Jeter $750,000 this past season when he led the league in
runs scored with 128, was fifth in hitting with a .324 average,
and was named to his first All-Star team. His 19 homers and
84 RBIs were career highs. His salary was $50,000 less than
utility infielder Luis Sojo.

Yet, the Yankees never gave Bernie Williams a multiyear
pact, and are now braced for their best all-around player to
split via free agency. As crazy as it seems to people inside and
out of the organization, the same thing could happen to Jeter
following the 2001 season. If George Steinbrenner learns

from the mistakes he made with Williams—and the Boss isn't a fool—by then Jeter could be a couple of years into being the next Yankee captain.

Already, his teammates talk about his leadership qualities in a room that's loaded with veterans. Beyond that, Frank Crosetti has ordained Jeter the best Yankee shortstop in sixty-six years.

"Right at the top," Crosetti said when asked where Jeter ranks among the Bomber shortstops he's seen since he started playing for the club in 1932.

Because he is wise beyond his twenty-four years, Jeter has been very careful not to step on the toes of David Cone, Paul O'Neill, Tino Martinez, Bernie Williams, Joe Girardi, Tim Raines, and Darryl Strawberry. As hard as it is to believe, the time is coming when that group of leaders won't be in pin-stripes. Aside from Williams's situation, O'Neill wants to play one more year, Cone can't pitch forever, Martinez is only signed through 2000, and Girardi, Raines, and Strawberry don't have contracts for next year.

Cone, the ultimate team leader, believes Jeter has the qualities to be the first Yankee captain since Don Mattingly left in 1995.

"He is a future captain in the making," Cone said of the shortstop who has both feet firmly planted on the ground and his head squarely attached to his shoulders, courtesy of the way he was raised. "He is way beyond his years in terms of maturity, and plays shortstop, which is a leader position. He certainly has the leadership qualities, and it looks like he will be here for a long time. He is a perfect fit at a very young age. He has experience in New York and has handled himself very well."

When the subject is mentioned to Jeter, a blank stare comes over his face.

"I don't know, I just go out and play," Jeter explained. "I am not the type of guy who will call a team meeting or something like that. You lead by example, and if that makes you a team leader, that's fine. I don't even know if we had a captain on my high school baseball team. I was the captain of the basketball team, but I can't remember about baseball."

In the storied history of the Yankees, they have had ten captains. Hal Chase was the first in 1912. After Mattingly left, the position has remained vacant, since Joe Torre knows he has more than enough veterans to take care of the leadership role. In between Chase and Mattingly, Babe Ruth, Lou Gehrig, Thurman Munson, Graig Nettles, Willie Randolph, and Ron Guidry have been named captains by managers. Gehrig's run of seven seasons is the longest. Ruth was captain for five days in 1922.

Randolph and Guidry were captains together from 1986 to 1989, so the third base coach knows what it takes.

"A team leader isn't a rah-rah guy," Randolph said. "You lead by going to the mat every day, playing hurt, and playing hard. I think Derek could be that guy. He isn't very vocal but he brings it every day."

Is there any better example that Jeter "brings it every day" than the way he runs out every ground ball? Even though he's in his third year, he long ago gained the veterans' respect.

"He is already on his way to being the main man here," Strawberry said. "The guy loves to play and knows how to play, and that's what establishes you as a leader. He knows what it's all about and he excels at it each and every day. He isn't afraid of failure. As a shortstop, he's a leader the way Cal Ripken was a leader when he played short."

Strawberry is aware that this Yankee team isn't built for a five-year run. He knows the day is coming when a clubhouse full of players will need Jeter to lean on.

"He's going to be around, and will have to show the other guys what winning is all about," Strawberry said.

Joe Girardi played with Andre Dawson, a man who every other team leader in baseball history is measured against. He sees the possibility of Jeter leading the same way Dawson did: quietly and by example.

"At twenty-four he is an important part of this clubhouse," Girardi said. "The dimension he brings is that he keeps everybody loose."

In Joe Torre's four managerial stops, he's had one captain—Bob Horner with the Braves.

"When you name a captain, you have to have a sense that nobody else will resent it," Torre said. "Sure Jeter could be one, because he has respect for the game and respect for his teammates."

And the respect of Crosetti, who was with the Yankees from 1932 to 1968 as a player and coach and wore the No. 2 Jeter sports.

"He makes plays I never could have even thought about," the eighty-seven-year-old Crosetti said while watching Jeter take ground balls during batting practice at Oakland Coliseum.

Shortstop is a Yankees position that hasn't been flooded with major talents. Phil Rizzuto was marvelous and so was Crosetti. But think about Jeter's predecessors: Tony Kubek, Bucky Dent, Roy Smalley, Wayne Tolleson, Gene Michael, Jim Mason, Bobby Meacham, Alvaro Espinoza, Rafael Santana, Andy Stankiewicz, Spike Owen, Mike Gallego, Tony Fernandez.

"He's hitting better this year, with more power," said Crosetti, whose last year as a player was 1948. "What I really like about him is that he is a nice kid who doesn't have a big head."

More than likely it won't be Torre who names Jeter the eleventh captain in Yankee history, since it won't be done for a couple of years, and by then Torre could be in a broadcast booth or in retirement, trying to decide if the 1996 or 1998 World Series ring matches what he is wearing.

When the day comes, Jeter will handle it like he does a ground ball to short in the ninth inning of a close game, because that's the number one reason Cone and Strawberry see him following Mattingly: he can play.

3

A Stay at Shea

On April 13 a steel expansion joint shook loose in the upper deck along the third base line at Yankee Stadium and destroyed the seat it fell upon. Had the joint fallen six hours later, during the game, it may well have had horrible consequences. At the time, though, only a handful of Anaheim Angels were at the Stadium for some early work, and nowhere near the damaged section. Fortunately, no one was hurt.

From the start of spring training, Steinbrenner had been relatively quiet about getting a new ballpark built for him by the city of New York. There was an occasional sentence or two about how the Yankees would never be a top draw playing where they are. About how Jacobs Field in Cleveland and Camden Yards in Baltimore—two of the Yankees biggest rivals on the playing field as well as in the free agent market—gave those teams an unfair advantage.

Then, just as the dust of the fallen joint settled, Steinbrenner and his City Hall ally, Mayor Rudolph Giuliani, had the new ballpark debate in high gear.

Yankee Stadium, ironically celebrating its seventy-fifth year, wasn't safe. On top of being in a bad neighborhood, there was now a chance a steel beam could fall on your head as you looked up to track a Bernie Williams fly to deep left-center. The Yankees, the mayor proposed, needed a new stadium, and said the site should be the West Side of Manhattan. Critics of the mayor said they wished he would respond as quickly to the crumbling schools, buildings, and roadways of the city. Meanwhile, Bronx Borough President Fernando Ferrer insisted that the Bronx, as the original home of the House that Ruth Built, was perfect for the Stadium, and has since proposed ways to renovate the Stadium and the surrounding area. There was no fast answer, though, and the controversy lingered over the course of the season, with the Boss ultimately saying that he didn't want to think about it until the season was over. There were more important things to do. Like winning.

The Yankees, who were riding a five-game win streak after taking three straight from the A's over the weekend, were itching to get back on the diamond. The game on April 13 against the Angels was postponed. So, too, was the next night's. For Hideki Irabu's benefit, the Yankees set up a game against Norwich, their Double-A affiliate, at Yankee Stadium, with no public admission.

The Yankees turned to the Mets for help, and an arrangement was made: the Yankees would play in Shea Stadium until Yankee Stadium was given a green light. There was a precedent: when the Stadium was rebuilt in 1972–76, the Yankees played two seasons in Shea (1974 and '75). The difference now was that the Yankee players would return to their grass-roots days of riding a bus in uniform.

Dress. Bus. Play. Bus home. Shower. All because the Mets had their own home series against the Cubs. It was far from perfect, but it beat sitting around for a third straight day wondering if the upper deck was ready to spit out any more beams.

Two blue and white Academy buses left Yankee Stadium at 9:20 in the morning and chugged north on Ruppert Place with a white NYPD car in front and a blue and white trailing. After wheezing at the curb, the caravan made a lazy left on 161st Street, then another left on Macombs Dam Drive as it motored toward the Major Deegan Expressway going south.

But this wasn't just another bus load of working stiffs trying to negotiate a morning commute. As the buses rolled down the entrance ramp, there was nothing but clear pavement ahead of them all the way to 138th Street since police had stopped southbound traffic. From there, with car 2815 running interference with its lights flashing, and the blue and white keeping curiosity seekers away behind the second bus, the Yankees made their way to one of the Triboro Bridge's EZ Pass lanes.

Now, all that was left of the highest-salaried bus ride in New York City history was for the drivers to navigate the Grand Central Parkway. When that was done without incident, the Yankees arrived safely at Shea.

Dressed in their uniforms, the seventeen-minute sojourn had all the trappings of a high school outing.

"The last time I was in this position, my mom washed my uniform," David Cone said.

The bizarre day got a little weirder when the Yankees departed the bus wearing their pinstriped pants and Yankee warm-up jackets outside Shea's press entrance and vanished into a sea of Yankee fans.

Since the Mets were using their clubhouse, the Bombers

lounged in the visitors' clubhouse, while the Angels occupied an auxiliary clubhouse behind the home dugout.

To make matters a bit more uncomfortable, it was raining. Batting practice was held indoors, and the Yankees did crossword puzzles and used the room with Cub uniforms hanging in the stalls to stretch their muscles.

Asked about the unique bus ride the Yankees wouldn't have to repeat until June 26, 27, and 28, when Baseball Armageddon arrived via an interleague series against the Mets, Cone said it was lively, "a circuslike atmosphere . . . definitely a New York type thing. We had the right attitude and it was a lot of fun."

With the monster of Yankee Stadium silenced, the Yankees didn't know what to expect from the fans when they arrived at Shea Stadium. And not having played since Sunday, and facing the prospect of having to perform under depressing gray skies and in a slight drizzle without a real batting practice, they didn't know what to expect from themselves. Furthermore, Ken Hill, a pitcher who had dominated them two weeks ago in California, was chucking for the Angels.

However, from the moment they exited the third-base dugout, all the Yankees had to do was close their eyes and they were back in the Bronx. As David Wells sauntered to the mound, Shea wasn't the Mets house, it was Yankee Stadium painted the wrong shade of blue.

"It was easy to concentrate because we had all those Yankee fans," Tino Martinez said following a 6–3 Yankee win that upped their winning streak to six and improved their record to 7–4. "When we took the field, they were loud. I was pumped up and ready to go. It was good, especially with the type of day it was."

When Joe Torre boarded the bus at Yankee Stadium

earlier that day, he had two questions dancing in his head: "Neither one had anything to do with where we were playing. I wanted to know about the two extra days [David] Wells was getting and the way we were going to hit the ball. The first inning settled that on both accounts."

Wells, who hadn't worked since April 7 and admits that idle time ranks up there with crash diets and last call as things he detests, faced the minimum eighteen Angels across six innings. The lone hit he allowed, a one-out single to Jim Edmonds in the second, was erased when Phil Nevin bounced into a 4–6–3 double play.

Chuck Knoblauch got the crowd of 40,743 rocking when he led off with a single to right. Derek Jeter moved Knoblauch to second with a perfect sacrifice bunt, and Paul O'Neill's single to center scored Knoblauch.

Darryl Strawberry, who finished with three hits to raise his average to a team-high .400, electrified the crowd with a bases-empty solo homer that reached the bleachers in left field, which upped the bulge to 6–0.

"Honest, I didn't try to write that script," said Strawberry, who couldn't have asked for a better return to a ballpark he used to own in his years with the Mets.

Following the victory, it was back on the bus and one more ride home through commuter traffic.

"It was worth it," Willie Banks said when the buses returned to the Stadium at 4:55 P.M. "Especially when you get a win."

While Steinbrenner praised the efforts of Giuliani and the city's team of inspectors, it was clear that the weekend series against the Tigers, when the Yankees planned to celebrate the Stadium's 75th birthday, wasn't going to be held in the Bronx.

Since the Yankees were slated to be in Detroit the following weekend, a plan was hatched to have the teams switch weekends. Because the Yankees are the home team's biggest draw at Tiger Stadium, the move made no sense from a financial standpoint. However, major league baseball stepped in and guaranteed the Tigers wouldn't lose any money in the deal.

What the toothless Tigers did lose were two of three, and needed Brian Moehler to hurl eight innings of one-run ball in order to beat Hideki Irabu, 2–1. The three-game series drew a paltry 38,719, or an average of 12,906.

By the time the Yankees opened a two-game series against the Blue Jays at the Stadium on April 27–28, they had forged a 14–5 record and were the talk of baseball. Yet, to Steinbrenner it made little difference. Yes, he was proud of certain players such as Hideki Irabu, Darryl Strawberry, and Scott Brosius, and the way the club had bounced back from a 1–4 start to win 13 of 14 for 14–5 record, which was the best in the A.L. and second best in the majors—this despite very little in the way of help from Bernie Williams, Paul O'Neill, Chuck Knoblauch, David Cone, and Mariano Rivera. Still, it wasn't even May.

Twenty-five years of owning the Yankees had taught Steinbrenner a lifetime of baseball lessons. He has worked hard to overcome a football mentality, to the point where an April loss isn't the end of the world and a win doesn't allow you to print World Series tickets.

Now, with his team the talk of the baseball galaxy, the Boss wanted to make sure the most recognizable hat in sports didn't increase even an eighth of an inch in size.

"There are some things that please me," the Boss told the *New York Post,* "but you have to please me beyond April. On the whole, I am very pleased but very cautious. If we don't focus on each and every game, we could be in trouble."

After praising his ballclub for overcoming El Niño on the West Coast and an ocean of distractions caused by a falling expansion joint in Yankee Stadium, the Boss made sure he wasn't going to be portrayed as overconfident.

"I have seen a lot of things happen to teams that get that way," he said, contacting the *Post* three times to make sure his message was loud and clear. "We have to carry it farther. The teams we have to beat are ahead of us in the schedule."

Like the Boston Red Sox. One month into the season, Boston's sizzling 16–6 start put them right on the heels of the Yankees.

"They have a good team, they are right there with us," Steinbrenner said of the Sox. "One of us will blink between the three of us. Maybe even four. Baltimore has a good team, and the Blue Jays, with that pitching, have a good club."

While Steinbrenner admitted to being pleasantly surprised by Brosius, Irabu, and Mike Stanton, he wasn't shocked with the way Strawberry bolted from the gate.

"Where are all the doomsayers now, the people who said we were crazy to bring him back?" the Boss said of his designated hitter, who led the team in homers (5), was batting .320, and had 13 RBIs. "Just like those people who said I was crazy for bringing Torre in. You don't hear from them now."

When Kenny Rogers was shipped to the A's for Brosius, Steinbrenner admitted he would have been flying blind on what he was getting back to play third base if not for scouting reports.

"Our scouts said he would give us great defense," he said. "If he could hit like he did in 1996, we would have a helluva guy. He's hitting over .300." (Actually, .299 at the time.)

"Whether that continues or not, I don't know. But he can play the bag as good as anybody we have had here since [Graig] Nettles."

Despite a lack of offense from Derek Jeter and Knoblauch, the Boss liked what he saw from his double play combination.

"They have been the key to our defense, they have really played well together," he said.

Like everybody else, Steinbrenner admired the job reliever Mike Stanton did filling in for Mariano Rivera.

"Stanton has been tremendous, but so have the other relievers. [Jeff] Nelson and the young man from Colorado [Darren Holmes], I took a look at his stats, and he gets better as the season goes on. He will be okay too."

By the time April moved into May the Yankees were 17–6, had survived a nightmare beginning and their ballpark falling apart. Still, the Boss knew there were more than five months remaining.

"We haven't won anything," he warned. "We better not be feeling too good about ourselves."

4

The Boomer Can Pitch

Of course, there's never any way to know if a pitcher is set to hurl a perfect game.

Electric stuff in the bullpen often turns into salad in the first inning and the pitcher is in the showers by the third. Salad in the bullpen is transformed into sensational stuff during the walk from the pen to the mound. Beyond that, perfection necessitates help from others, and most of all, an ocean of luck.

So naturally, nobody in the Yankee Stadium crowd of 49,820—many on hand to grab a free Beanie Baby—was thinking David Wells was about to make history against the feeble Minnesota Twins on May 17.

Yes, Wells was 4–1 when he climbed the mound on a crystal clear afternoon. But his ERA was a hefty 5.23, and it was only eleven days since Joe Torre questioned Wells's conditioning after the veteran lefty failed to hold a nine-run lead in the searing Texas heat on May 6.

All winter the questions surrounding the Yankees starting rotation were asked often, and they were legitimate. Would David Cone's surgically repaired right shoulder hold up? Would Hideki Irabu shed the label of $12.8 million bust? Was Andy Pettitte's back okay?

How about Wells? According to Torre, Wells had become the Home Office for Bad Body Language at the first sign that things weren't going his way.

An umpire would miss a pitch and Wells would mope. Another missed pitch and more moping. Finally, frustrated, Wells would groove a pitch and watch it get crushed. More than one person noticed Wells looking to the dugout for an early out through his first season in pinstripes. While he talked about being a gamer and battler, there were nights when Wells was neither.

Despite winning a career-high sixteen games, Wells had to fight off Dwight Gooden over the final month of 1997 to secure a spot in Torre's rotation for the A.L. Division Series against the Indians.

Now, Wells had melted for the first time in 1998. And Torre, who rarely knocks a player in public, was annoyed. Only the Yankees stuffing a wild 15–13 win over the Rangers into their luggage thanks to five RBIs from Derek Jeter and homers by Chuck Knoblauch, Paul O'Neill, Tim Raines, and Jeter took the sting out of what Torre saw from Wells in Arlington.

Giving up seven runs in the third, which shaved the lead to 9–7, was one thing. And Wells's flipping Torre the ball and not looking at him when he was hooked wasn't a major sin. But reacting the way he did when things started to unravel was something else, and Torre didn't like to see it.

"No, it wasn't fun," Torre said of a 9–0 lead after two innings. "A manager likes to get a big lead, but I was never comfortable. I didn't like the way Wells was on the mound. He was walking around kicking stuff."

For Torre, that is about as far as he goes in criticizing a player. But he took another step and challenged the party animal to work harder in between starts. Asked why Wells melted in the 92 degree heat that turned the Ballpark in Arlington into a sauna, Torre attacked the question head on:

"I thought his stuff was good, I just thought he ran out of gas. Maybe he's not in shape."

Following a meeting in Minneapolis between Wells, Torre, and pitching coach Mel Stottlemyre, the trio said they understood each other. Wells viewed the early hook as a sign that his manager and pitching coach had lost confidence in him. In turn, the bosses wanted the bad body language to stop immediately. Torre never said it publicly, but even in early May he knew he needed Wells's talented—and durable—left arm if the Yankees were going to have a season to remember.

As usual, when things didn't go Wells's way, he boycotted the writers. As if they had anything to do with Torre's comments beyond listening to them, writing them down, and putting them in the paper. But by now everybody was used to the drill.

To his credit, Wells bounced back from the Texas Disaster by beating the Royals 3–2 at Yankee Stadium on May 12. In eight innings he allowed two runs, five hits, and fanned nine.

Five days later, after pitching against the Twins, he would transform New York City, a town Wells should have owned long before throwing a perfect game, into "Boomer's World."

As is his custom before every game, Torre never goes to the bullpen to watch his starter warm up. That duty belongs to Stottlemyre, the veteran pitching coach Torre relies heavily on. One of Torre's biggest strengths is listening to his coaches. They are not subjects, they are not beneath him. Where managers such as Lou Piniella are reputed to be brutal on coaches, a trait he may have picked up playing for Billy Martin, Torre relies on the information tank.

"When Mel came out of the bullpen, I asked him how Wells was doing," Torre recalled later. "He just said, 'Wow.'"

Again, nasty stuff beyond the left-field fence often means nothing. And nothing about the first inning was sensational. Wells retired Matt Lawton on a fly ball to left, Brent Gates on a fly to center, and future Hall of Famer Paul Molitor on a routine grounder to the right side.

With one out in the second, Wells gave an indication that the electric stuff he had shown Stottlemyre and catcher Jorge Posada in the bullpen had made the trip to the mound. He blew a high-octane fastball by Ron Coomer. On the bench, David Cone made note of the unhittable pitch.

After Wells fanned John Shave and Javier Valentin, looking, and got Pat Meares to swing through a change-up in the third, trained eyes knew if Wells was ever going to throw a no-hitter, this would be the day.

"You could tell by then that his stuff was unbelievable," Cone said.

Two fly balls surrounded a strikeout of Gates in the fourth. Meanwhile, Bernie Williams's two-out homer off LaTroy Hawkins in the home fourth gave Wells a 2–0 lead to work with. The way Wells was throwing, that two-run advantage seemed like a double-digit lead in the Twins dugout.

Wells fanned Marty Cordova looking and Coomer swinging to start the fifth, and ended it by inducing Alex Ochoa to bounce out to the right side.

Now it was serious. Fifteen batters and not a sniff of a base hit. And it didn't appear a razor-sharp Wells was going to suddenly lose sight of the plate with his fastball, curveball, slider, or change-up.

Jorge Posada, the switch-hitting catcher who was progressing every day defensively, knew he was on the other end of something special after Wells got through the fifth.

"With all his pitches working, you knew he was at the top of his game," Posada said.

By the time Wells was ready to work the sixth, the Stadium had warmed to the occasion. The upper reaches of the storied ballpark couldn't tell via the naked eye that Wells's stuff was exceptional. But if they were paying attention, they saw the anemic swings the Twins were getting on Wells. And they had no trouble seeing the scoreboard in left-center that had a zero under the H on the Twins line score.

As is baseball custom, the Yankees said next to nothing to Wells in the dugout.

Cone pulled a jacket up around his face. Wells disappeared into the clubhouse between innings. The players had become just like the people in the seats: they knew they had a chance to see history.

Two more strikeouts preceded Wells getting Meares to fly out to Williams in center for the third out of the sixth. Forgotten afterward was the simple fact that the Yankees hadn't done much with Hawkins through six innings. Darryl Strawberry doubled in the second, moved to third on a passed ball, and scored on a wild pitch. Then there was Williams's homer in the fourth, and that was it. So, while Wells flirted with history, he did so with just a two-run lead. It may have looked larger in the Twins dugout, but it wasn't much on the scoreboard.

Lawton flied out and Gates grounded out to start the seventh. Now it was Molitor, a .400 (16–for–40) hitter against Wells coming into the game. Wells had gone to 3–0 on Lawton in the fourth and battled back to get him on a fly to Chad Curtis in left. But Molitor was different. At forty-one, his batting eye was keen, his compact swing still lethal, and now he had Wells in a 3–1 hole.

Respecting Molitor, Wells painted the outside corner with a strike. At 3–2, he went along with Posada's call for a two-seam fastball that Molitor swung through.

"He went 3–0 on Lawton, but when he went 3–1 on Molitor, that's probably the one memory I'll take from this game," Torre said. "When he got Molly, I thought he was going to pitch no-hitter."

An RBI double by Strawberry and an RBI single by Curtis in the seventh supplied Wells with a 4–0 bulge and lightened the pressure of winning the game.

When Cordova stepped in to start the eighth, Yankee Stadium was in a deep throat roar. Six outs were all that stood between Wells and perfection. Now the crowd inhaled and exhaled on every pitch.

Cordova grounded out to Jeter before Coomer spanked a fastball right at Knoblauch, who knocked it down and had plenty of time to throw Coomer out. Wells put himself three outs away from perfection by getting Ochoa on a foul pop to Tino Martinez.

By the time Wells moved toward the mound for the ninth, the Stadium was ear-splitting loud. And by now, throughout the city, neighborhoods had flocked to the television and car radios were turned to WABC. It was one of those special moments that you knew where you were for the final three outs.

"I was hoping the fans would kind of shush a little bit,"

Wells said afterward. "They were making me nervous."

Shave flied out to Paul O'Neill for the first out. Two more to go. Valentin fanned. One more to go. Only Meares, the No. 9 hitter in the lineup and the twenty-seventh batter Wells faced, stood between Wells and the only regular season perfect game in Yankee history.

A fly to right had O'Neill moving toward the foul line. As Wells moved off the mound, his eyes never left the ball. When it settled in O'Neill's glove, Wells pumped his left arm until it looked like it would fall off.

As the Stadium rocked, Wells was mobbed by his teammates. Willie Banks and Strawberry hoisted him on their shoulders, and Wells waved his cap at the fans who now had ticket stubs as proof they were part of history.

The fans wouldn't let the moment go. Wells disappeared into the dugout but returned for a curtain call.

"The New York people see he is a blue-collar guy," Torre said. "And the rough edges make them like him even more than anything else. But the Boomer can pitch."

That has never been the question with Wells. More than anything else, it's been his attitude. But in addition to being perfect on the mound, Wells was perfect off it. He credited Posada, whom he shook off only twice, and his mates. In dedicating the historic moment to his late mother Ann, Wells showed an emotional side that not many see.

"Nobody can take it from me, ever," he said, as if anybody would want to pry a perfect game from him. "No matter what happens the rest of my life, I am honored. I wish a few more people could have been here to see it. But in my heart and mind, my mom is with me."

More in tune with the long Yankee history than any other Yankee, Wells understood that along with Don

Larsen, he will forever be connected to the lore for being perfect.

"There is a special place in my heart for what I did today," he said after throwing the fifteenth perfect game in baseball history, and the first no-hitter by a Yankee since Dwight Gooden turned the trick against the Mariners on May 14, 1996. Wells was the tenth Yankee hurler to throw a no-hitter. "I am happy I did it in pinstripes."

George Steinbrenner sent a bottle of Dom Pérignon champagne to the clubhouse. As the night progressed, Wells and teammates celebrated at Dorian's on the Upper East Side. The next day he played in a charity golf tournament set up by Stottlemyre, then appeared on the *Late Show with David Letterman*. Tuesday, Wells was honored at City Hall by Mayor Guiliani, who presented him with the key to the city.

"Is this a good idea?" Wells joked.

Hours after the City Hall ceremony, Wells was telling reporters that the *Post*'s Joel Sherman, a baseball columnist Wells doesn't talk to, found a way to rip him in the paper. Standing nearby, Cone came to Sherman's defense and said the piece wasn't negative. The theme of Sherman's column was that hopefully the gem would be the springboard to Wells growing up a little. As it turned out, the perfect game was a springboard to a career year.

For one gorgeous spring day, Wells put New York in the palm of his meaty left hand. For every guy who wanted to tell his boss to stuff it, for every guy who always wanted to do it his way, Wells was the man. For one day, he was everybody's hero.

Yankee Profile:
David Cone

By the time David Cone took the ball for real on April 4, the Yankees were 0–2 and Yankee fans were in a full-blown panic. Andy Pettitte and David Wells had already lost and now it was up to Cone's talented but surgically repaired right arm to get the Yankees in the win column against the A's at the Oakland Coliseum.

Cone was supposed to pitch the night before, but rain washed that assignment out. Like everybody else, he was anxious to see how the wing held up. Arthroscopic surgery in October had cleaned up the rotator cuff area of the shoulder, and Cone was so strict about his rehab process that he found time to throw while on a cruise in the middle of the Atlantic Ocean. By December he was so far along in the program that he stayed in Tampa for the holidays. When spring training opened, Cone was clearly the farthest along of any pitcher in camp.

There had been a few bumps in the road; a slightly sprained ankle and a day or two when he couldn't get the shoulder as loose as he would have liked. But for a pitcher the Yankees hadn't expected to be ready before May, or possibly June, everybody was excited about Cone's progress.

His right shoulder had been invaded by a surgeon's scalpel twice in the past two years. Before the flesh and muscles were sliced and structural problems corrected, the wing had propelled thousands of pitches, which extracted a tremendous toll and left people wondering how much remained in one of

David Wells pitches his way to a perfect game on March 17. It was the first regular-season perfect game in Yankee history. *(Photo by Nury Hernandez/New York Post)*

A strange sight—the Yankees take the field at Shea Stadium on April 15. They were forced to play there after a beam fell at Yankee Stadium. *(Photo by Charles Wenzelberg/New York Post)*

Joe Girardi leaps into the air trying to make a play at home. He and Jorge Posada were a seamless platoon behind the plate. *(Photo by Charles Wenzelberg/New York Post)*

Teammates charge the field to defend Tino Martinez, who was beaned by Baltimore reliever Armando Benitez, leading to an ugly brawl. *(Photo by Charles Wenzelberg/*New York Post)

Paul O'Neill had a predictably strong season and is an anchor in the Yankees lineup. *(Photo by Charles Wenzelberg/*New York Post)

Orlando "El Duque" Hernandez gets his first start—and win—against the Devil Rays on June 3. He took the mound for David Cone, whose hand was bitten by a dog. *(Photo by Nury Hernandez/New York Post)*

Derek Jeter's outstanding play with his glove and bat, as well as his leadership in the clubhouse, have made him a candidate for next Yankee captain. *(Photo by Nury Hernandez/New York Post)*

Chuck Knoblauch turns a double play in May. Disappointed in his season, Knoblauch has also had off-the-field concerns, including his father's battle with Alzheimer's. *(Photo by Nury Hernandez/*New York Post)

A frustrated Andy Pettitte against Toronto in September. Always self-critical, he was especially hard on himself as he struggled through the end of the season. *(Photo by Charles Wenzelberg/New York Post)*

The sweet stroke of Bernie Williams earns him the American League batting title with a .339 average. *(Photo by Nury Hernandez /New York Post)*

David Cone's amazing twenty wins were the best of the staff and made him a candidate for the Cy Young Award. Any doubts about his shoulder's strength and stamina were erased. *(Photo by Francis Specker/New York Post)*

The legendary 1927 New York Yankees, including the mythic Lou Gehrig and Babe Ruth, the standard by which all other Yankee teams were measured, held the team record for most wins at 110. The 1998 Yankees bested that by four wins. (*Courtesy of the Baseball Hall of Fame Library*)

the best baseball arms ever. But since the shoulder belonged to Cone, the immediate feeling in the Yankees universe was that he would be all right.

So when the Yankees were cruising with a three-run lead in the fifth inning against the hapless A's, there wasn't a pin-striped uniform who didn't believe that Cone's first outing of the season was headed for triumph. One inning later, though, the Yankees trailed by four and were on their way to an embarrassing 7–3 loss. For the first time since 1985 the Yankees had opened the season with three straight defeats.

"Most definitely," Tim Raines said when asked if he thought the lead was in perfect hands. "He was throwing the ball well. Even when he got in trouble, you expected him to get out of it, but it didn't happen."

According to Cone, it didn't happen because of the 0–1 cut fastball to Scott Spiezio that didn't cut and landed beyond the right-field wall for a grand slam in the sixth. Or the 1–2 sidearm slider to Rickey Henderson in the fifth that Henderson drove to left for a two-run single, the fatal bullet.

No, what killed Cone were three walks. And since all three scored, Cone, as always, was correct.

"The slider to Rickey was a bad pitch, and the cutter to Spiezio was in his wheelhouse," said Cone, who gave up seven runs and seven hits in 5 1/3 innings. "But the walks were the key to the big innings."

Cone walked rookie A.J. Hinch after Spiezio doubled leading off the fifth. Both scored on Henderson's single. In the sixth, Cone walked Kevin Mitchell after just missing with a 1–2 pitch. His four-pitch walk to Jason Giambi loaded the bases for Spiezio.

"I let him get away," Cone said of Giambi. "But the other two [walks] I was ahead of them. I felt great and I was real pleased with the way I started off. Then I let it get away from me. That's disappointing."

So too was the 0–3 beginning to a season many believed would be a stroll in the park for the Bombers.

"I wanted to stop it today," Cone said. "Everybody in here feels like we're going to come back."

Always one of the most analytical of pitchers, Cone wasn't wild about facing the same team in consecutive starts. Even if it was the "Triple A's." So he took the mound for the home opener on April 10 with a certain amount of trepidation.

Five runs by the A's in the second made Cone appear to be just another pitcher in the watered-down market of arms that the major leagues have become. Before the fifth was out, Cone was gone from a game the Yankees would win, 17–13.

Because he is Cone, the crowd of 56,717 gave him a rousing ovation as he jogged to the dugout. But there was another question added to the Yankees galaxy. In two starts he was 0–1 with a ridiculous ERA of 14.90. And it was against the A's, a team that would be out of the A.L. West race before school was out.

"It was a great game, the Giants beat the Raiders. What the hell," Cone quipped of the four-hour, six-minute marathon that belonged in the Tavern League. "There are no excuses from where I stand. I have been awful the last two starts. The team has given me leads and I haven't been able to hold them. The offense refused to let us lose. If we had lost that game, I would have been the most miserable man on earth."

In addition to the teams combining for thirty runs, the most scored at the Stadium since June 3, 1933, ten pitchers were raked for 32 hits and issued 18 walks. A dozen of them were to the Yankees. A's starter Jimmy Haynes walked five in 2 1/3 innings, and Aaron Small issued four passes in one inning.

"I feel great, but what has happened is that I get into trouble and I go into a panic mode," Cone said.

Since Cone had been getting ahead of hitters, nobody believed he was hurt. However, what he was doing when he was ahead in the count was a cause for concern. Four times he gave up a hit with a 1–2 offering.

"It's been a problem," he admitted. "When I've been ahead, I haven't been able to put hitters away. I haven't been able to finish hitters off."

Fortunately for the Yankees, they had enough muscle to make sure Cone didn't finish them off in their home opener.

Maybe it was the ERA of 10.57 next to his name after his third start. Or the embarrassing .368 average hitters were raking against him. Then again it could be the numbness in the right hand. Possibly, at thirty-five, with two shoulder surgeries in as many years, David Cone knew that a brilliant career was a lot closer to the finish line than many cared to admit. Whatever the reason, he was thinking about his past and future as he battled to straighten out his present.

Having earned more than $32 million since 1990, Cone recalled a time when he was a tapped out nineteen-year-old minor leaguer in Charleston, South Carolina. In the next breath, he began to formulate plans for retirement, a life after baseball, when his right arm told him the clock had run out on a fascinating New York career.

"Something with the [Players] Association, working with the licensing program," Cone said.

Clearly, those first weeks of the 1998 season provided strange days for Cone, who has experienced more than a few bizarre days and nights since leaving Kansas City as an eighteen-year-old in 1981.

He knew the Yankees were counting on him. Then he looked at his first three starts and shook his head. He was tired of checking the forecast to see if it would be warm enough for his right hand to feel the ball. Plain and simple, he was groping like never before.

"My whole goal was to be reliable, and I haven't done that," Cone said. "I need to get my act together."

Next, on April 18, Cone won at Detroit and evened his record at 1–1. But he had to struggle to beat the Tigers. "A lot of guts and real smart," George Steinbrenner said of his performance.

But his outing hadn't been impressive, which made his next outing, at Yankee Stadium on April 24, also against the Tigers, a crossroads outing. Face it, if he was Willie Banks, Cone wouldn't have been in the rotation. If he was Willie Banks, Cone would have been downloaded from the Yankees mainframe. But he was David Cone, a pitcher blessed with an electric arm whose best weapons have always been his head and heart.

When he was eighteen, Cone wasn't all that smart with money. When it was time to report to Charleston in 1982, every penny of the $17,000 signing bonus the Royals gave him the summer before had vanished. Some to his parents. Some was blown. None of it was put aside for taxes, a mistake the IRS reminded him of four years later.

"It's a long time ago, but I remember it pretty good," Cone said. "Sleeping on the floor with my clothes rolled up and used as a pillow. We were eating peanut butter and jelly sandwiches. I remember the apartment. Our next door neighbors threw out an old love seat. We took it out of the garbage, had it fumigated, and took turns sleeping on it. Made $2,000 for the whole year."

Of course, Cone's career turned out better than his roommate, John Bryant. He died like so many others do: arm trouble on the back roads of the Single A circuit.

Now, Cone tried to beg his wing for more life to put away hitters. Joe Torre suggested that the Yankees should accept what Cone was giving and move on. After all, Cone wasn't supposed to be ready until May. Still, it was David Cone. And if you were surprised by the confusion in his face, how do you think he felt?

Conceding that his "Make It Up as I Go Along" method of pitching taxed his shoulder, since he goes at hitters from every imaginable angle, Cone attempted to smooth out his delivery. He went back to his signature hesitation. It might rob the shoulder of life, but the fire that burns in Cone's belly was overruled by the Shoulder Police in Cone's head.

"If it takes something out of my arm, so be it," Cone said. "But I am not going out there and getting my [butt] kicked. That was getting old to watch."

To those who watched it, it was inconceivable that he would reach 200 innings. At that barrier, a $5.5 million option becomes his call instead of the Yankees, who can buy him out for $1.5 million if they fail to pick up the option that's theirs if Cone falls short of 200.

As always, he would give it his best and battle because he is Cone. He would go after hitters with sidearm sliders, split-fingered fastballs, cut fastballs, and a nanosecond hesitation in the delivery. He would be Cone because he doesn't know any other way but to fight every hitter every inch of the way. That attitude helped him survive Charleston poverty.

Slowly, Cone began to come out of it. After he beat the Tigers in Detroit on April 18 for his first win, he beat them again six days later. As the winning streak grew to seven, Cone was going six and seven innings. Then, on June 7 against the Marlins at the Stadium, Cone, who had missed his last start due to a scratch on the inside of his right index finger thanks to his mother's dog, Veronica, went lights out. A single to Jeff Zaun in the third and a double to Todd Dunwoody in the eighth were the only hits he gave up in a 4–1 victory. The winning streak was at eight, the record at 8–1, and the ERA reduced to 4.97.

For all the cynics who said Cone had been so brilliant against the hitting-impaired Marlins, he answered by dominating the muscle-bound Indians in his next start. In eight innings he allowed one run and eight hits to post a 4–2 victory. The Indians would get him in the next outing, pinning a 7–4 loss on him that stopped the streak at nine.

If there were any questions remaining, Cone answered them across the next seven starts, when he went 6–1.

On July 28 he beat the Angels 9–3, allowing one earned run in seven innings to run his record to 15–3, the first fifteen-game winner in the A.L. for the season. After a long sixth inning, Cone went to Joe Torre and Mel Stottlemyre and informed them that his valuable right arm was a little stiff. There was some concern, and it fueled the fires of the Yankee trade talks with the Mariners for Randy Johnson.

Ultimately, though, it turned out to be nothing. Cone won three of his next four outings, and by the middle of August he was 18–4, on pace to hit the 200-inning cash register. Now people were talking about his winning twenty and possibly adding a Cy Young to his trophy case.

Two no-decisions, three losses, and one win in Cone's next six starts put him in a position where he needed to work at least five innings and hope the Yankees were leading when he exited in his final regular season tuneup.

That's exactly what happened. Cone went seven innings, threw 101 pitches, and beat the Devil Rays 3–1. At 20–7, he had won twenty games ten years apart, to break the record for the longest stretch between twenty-win seasons. Since Cone had lost his previous two starts, he'd resigned himself that a twenty-win season was done. Given a final chance, he'd turned the trick. And in the process he threw 207 2/3 innings, to gain control of his option and future.

Standing in the Yankee clubhouse after the milestone victory, Cone was certainly proud of the achievement. But when Joe Girardi presented him with the ball and a hug, tears flowed from eyes that have seen almost everything in baseball.

"I was okay," Cone said. "Until Joe did that. Then I got real emotional. It was something special."

That was a good way to describe it, because Cone has always been special. On the mound. In the clubhouse. And every other place where baseball business has been conducted.

David Wells was the Yankees best pitcher from start to finish. Derek Jeter was the Yankees MVP. But make no mistake, Cone was the guts of the best team in baseball. In good times and bad.

5

Birds and Beanballs

Only in the Yankees universe could the fifteenth perfect game in major league history be reduced to an afterthought in forty-eight hours. In other cities, the glow of such an accomplishment would linger for weeks. Thanks to an Orioles reliever by the name of Armando Benitez, nobody was talking about Wells's Sunday gem by late Tuesday night, May 19.

Instead of Wells, the talk shifted to one of the most vicious baseball fights in history. Juan Marichal hitting John Roseboro over the head with a bat in the 1960s and an all-day brawl between the Braves and Padres in the 1980s ranked higher on the Serious Meter. However, in a day and age where the players are tight union brothers, often represented by the same agents, when they play in each other's charity golf outings and constantly fraternize with each other around the batting cage, what transpired on May 19 was certainly surprising. And scary.

The Orioles, already eleven games behind the Bombers, visited the Bronx for what was for them a critical series. Down 5–4, the Yankees sent Bernie Williams to the plate to face Benitez with two men on. Williams proceeded to crush a colossal home run that would have landed on the Grand Concourse if it hadn't collided with a seat in the upper deck of right field. The blast, Williams's fourth of the season, gave the Yankees a 7–5 advantage.

Next up was Tino Martinez. What no one except perhaps Martinez himself was thinking was a similar situation three years ago. In 1995, when Tino was with the Mariners, Benitez walked the bases loaded and gave up a grand slam to Edgar Martinez. The next pitch ended up in Tino's back.

Unfortunately, this time things were no different. Benitez's next pitch, a fastball that had been clocked as high as 100 mph, drilled Tino Martinez in the back. To make matters worse, when Benitez saw Darryl Strawberry leading a slow-moving band of Bombers toward the mound from the first-base dugout, he foolishly threw his glove down and welcomed the Yankees to come get him with his arms.

After Graeme Lloyd raced in from the bullpen and went after Benitez, the action drifted toward the third-base dugout, where Scott Brosius attempted to take the frightened reliever down with a head-first tackle. From there Benitez ran down the steps and headed to the clubhouse when Strawberry unloaded a vicious left-hand punch. That resulted in the Yankee slugger getting socked under the left eye by Oriole reliever Alan Mills as three other Orioles pinned Strawberry to the ground.

"I have never been that frightened in a long time," said Yankee starter David Cone, who went six innings, gave up five runs and seven hits, and left trailing, 5–1. "I saw Darryl in a bad way with four or five guys on top of him. It was scary." Cone called it the most serious baseball fight he had ever seen.

When order was restored, Mills, Benitez, Lloyd, Jeff Nelson, and Strawberry were ejected.

Of course, there was still a game that needed to be played. Tim Raines stepped up to face former Yankee Bobby Munoz. Rock wasted no time and sent Munoz's first pitch into the right-field bleachers for the final two runs and a Yankee 9–5 victory.

"That was the way to do it," Joe Torre said of Raines's third homer, which sent a juiced-up crowd of 31,311 into a frenzy.

But Torre was angry about the beanball incident. "How can I say this without cursing?" he wanted to know. "It was a real rotten thing to do. Benitez caused a riot. He came within a foot of hitting Tino in the head."

GM Brian Cashman added, "That was the most chicken-shit thing I have ever seen."

According to George Steinbrenner, the bruise on Martinez's back was a large one. The Boss, who was livid about Benitez's actions, wasn't sure if Martinez would be sidelined by the drilling.

Derek Jeter, who bounced around trying to offer teammates protection during the twenty-minute donnybrook, questioned Benitez's IQ.

"That was the dumbest thing I have ever seen," said Jeter, who extended his hitting streak to fourteen games with a first-inning single. "If you ask anyone in baseball, they wouldn't disagree. That was dumb. It's not like Bernie showed him up going around the bases. It was dumb."

Even the low-key Williams showed emotion in talking about the incident, which wasn't soon forgotten by anybody who witnessed it.

"If I had a bad day, I am not going to throw a

hundred-mile-an-hour fastball and possibly hit somebody in the head," Williams said. "You can kill somebody."

"You have a guy who gave up a home run, and he has to take responsibility for that," Cashman said. "Hopefully, he will be suspended for that."

Curiously, Oriole manager Ray Miller apologized to Torre for Benitez's actions, prompting some Orioles to wonder what the first-year manager was doing. Take Benitez aside and tell him he was wrong. But apologizing to your archrival in the A.L. East?

"Why apologize?" an Oriole asked in disgust. "Sure, Benitez was wrong and all that. But did you see Strawberry come across and sucker punch Benitez? I don't see anybody from the Yankees apologizing to us for what Strawberry did. He has a reputation as a cheap-shot artist, and we're apologizing for what we're doing!"

"If I had to, of course I would," said Strawberry, when asked if he would fire another blast at Benitez's head. "I would do it again if I had to."

He added, "That wasn't cheap. Somebody had to get him. What were we supposed to do, let it go? When he threw his glove down, that's like a slap in the face."

Two days later A.L. president Gene Budig handed out the punishment. Benitez got benched for eight games and fined $2,000. For overly aggressive behavior, fighting, and prolonging the brawl, Budig suspended Strawberry and Lloyd for three games each and fined them $1,000. Nelson and Mills were docked $500 each and suspended for two games.

"I have talked with the managers and GM from both teams and have consulted with umpire Drew Coble," Budig said. "I have reviewed videotape submissions as well as crew chief Coble's report on the incident. Everyone agrees that player safety is our first concern, and we are all concerned to see that there is not a reoccurrence. This was a highly unfortunate and extremely dangerous on-field incident. The severity of the discipline reflects the gravity of the offenses. Mr. Benitez not only intentionally threw at Martinez, but the location of the pitch was extremely dangerous and could have seriously injured the player."

The Yankees agreed that Martinez could have suffered a career-ending injury, that's why they were livid about Benitez's punishment: they belived Benitez got off light.

"I want to get it behind us, number one," George Steinbrenner said. "Dr. Budig made the decision and I don't want to match wits with Dr. Budig as an academician. I don't know if he ever wore a jockstrap, but I have respect for him as an academician."

But the Boss did remark that he wasn't wild about losing Strawberry's lethal bat and two very effective relievers. And he went on to say, "What I am disappointed in is that we don't understand in baseball where the blame has to go. It's not always who gets involved in the fighting. You can't have guys throwing at players . . . I think a month would have been the least, but I am not Dr. Budig."

Naturally, Budig supported his decision. "I did what I thought was right," he said. "They are stiff and fair penalties."

Not to Brian Cashman, they weren't. "I thought [Benitez's punishment] should have been more," the Yankees GM said. "He acted first and we responded. It's tough. Our guys did what they had to do."

Meanwhile, so concerned about Benitez's fragile psyche were the Orioles that they left him at the team hotel for the game on May 20 while they continued to distance themselves from him.

"He is an immature young kid, he was out of control," manager Ray Miller said. "It goes totally against the tradition of the Baltimore Orioles."

Meanwhile, Tino Martinez felt the effects of the injury. He didn't play the next two nights against the Orioles, which were incident-free. Martinez returned Friday night in Boston and went 2–for–4. However, on a slide into third base, he aggravated the sore spot near the right shoulder blade.

Martinez missed the next six games and went home from Boston to New York for an MRI on May 25. It was done more for his peace of mind than anything else. And while the test came back clean, the numbers suggested Martinez was being bothered by it.

When Benitez beaned Martinez, he was hitting .326 with six homers and 37 RBIs in 38 games. By June 10, Martinez's batting average was at .299 and he had nine homers and 46 RBIs in fifty games. By the end of the month Martinez was at .265 and clearly not himself. As expected, he refused to use the sore shoulder blade as an excuse, but how could it not affect him?

Despite Benitez telling people he'd apologized to Martinez, Martinez said he never received a call, letter, fax, or telegram from the pitcher.

While the teams were on their best behavior in the two games immediately following the brawl, less than a month later in Baltimore the sores were reopened when Mike Stanton hit Eric Davis.

On June 15, brought in to relieve David Wells in the

seventh inning with the Yankees trailing 5–4, Stanton retired Joe Carter and Harold Baines before Rafael Palmeiro drove the first pitch over the right-center-field fence. When Davis couldn't get out of the way of a running fastball and it hit him, plate umpire John Hirschbeck immediately ejected Stanton.

Hirschbeck said the events of May 19 had a definite bearing on his decision.

Mike Stanton defended himself. "I think what happened in New York was a fluke," he said. "Things like that don't happen very often. But I have been in the league long enough for people to know that I am not a head-hunter."

Stanton, who had hit four batters in 31 1/3 innings, called the Orioles clubhouse to check on Davis's condition and to offer an apology.

Later, Davis told Strawberry, a close friend from their days in L.A., that he didn't believe Stanton was head-hunting.

Despite the parallels to the Benitez incident right down to Martinez and Palmeiro wearing the same No. 24 and getting hit in the middle of the digits, the Yankees were convinced Stanton wasn't throwing at Davis.

"As far as I am concerned, I won't be talking to the [A.L.] office because there isn't anything to talk about unless they have changed the game of baseball," GM Brian Cashman said. "If there are [disciplinary measures] I would be in shock. Our guy didn't call out the entire dugout like their guy did. There were a whole bunch of things their guy did."

One day later Budig partly appeased the Orioles and shocked the Yankees by suspending Stanton for five games and fining him $1,000. The Birds, who conveniently forgot how manager Ray Miller had hung Benitez out to dry, were looking for the same eight-game suspension Benitez got.

"I don't think it was justified," said Stanton, who filed an appeal immediately. "This is a situation that is totally separate from what happened in New York. I didn't expect anything because I knew what was going through my mind, and it wasn't hitting Eric Davis."

According to Budig, the incidents three weeks apart were related.

"I was appalled by the dangerous act by Mike Stanton," Budig said. "Especially in view of the recent and high profile brawl involving the Yankees and Orioles."

Budig's choice of words was amusing to Steinbrenner.

"I had to chuckle at Dr. Budig saying he was appalled," the Boss said. "It sounds like something issued by an educator and a college professor, and that is what he is. I am not taking issue with it. He is the American League president at the time and I respect his position. Whether he is the right man for the job . . . I like Budig, he is a nice man. He is an educator with a briefcase . . . The penalty didn't fit the crime."

Budig, who didn't talk to Stanton or Davis before making his decision, said he leaned heavily on umpire John Hirschbeck's report. While Torre and Stanton said they didn't believe Hirschbeck thought Stanton intentionally drilled Davis, Hirschbeck's report indicated otherwise.

"My report was cut and dried," Hirschbeck said. "I told him it was the first pitch after a homer and it wasn't like a breaking ball hit him in the foot. It was a fastball right between the numbers."

Nobody in pinstripes was taking the news that the

late inning lefty was going to be sidelined for five games without comment.

"I am very shocked, I disagree with it and I don't understand it," GM Brian Cashman said. "I certainly respect the league president but I think he missed on this one."

So did Torre, who hinted that Budig's lack of baseball experience didn't allow him to make the proper call.

"It's tough to make a rational decision when you don't have a feel for it," Torre said. "I don't want to say you don't know nothing about it. I say it's more of a feel thing. When you're not involved in the game and you're sitting on the sidelines and you have to make a decision, you take all the circumstances into account even though they don't apply. I'm sure he thought hard about the decision, but I thought it was harsh.

"There are a lot of things that don't make sense when you look at the big picture.

"Sure, if you read about it in the paper and look at the box score, then that's why this doesn't surprise me. You have to have a feel for the game to make evaluations that people have to live with."

Stanton lost his appeal and sat out from July 3 to July 10, and since the All-Star break was in the middle of the benching, many pointed to the inactivity to explain the miserable second half for a key cog in the Yankee bullpen.

6

Juggernaut

By the time May turned into June, there was very little doubt that if injuries didn't require body casts, the Yankees were on their way to winning the A.L. East for the second time in three years and would be appearing in the postseason for the fourth straight season.

You watched the Yankees every day from the middle of April to the end of May and you knew injury was the only way they weren't going to win it.

On May 24 the bosses at the *Post* cringed when the following lead appeared under my byline after the Yankees had outscored the Red Sox 26–7 in the final two games of a three-game series at Fenway: The A.L. East race is over!

Careful, they said. Still four months to go. Of course, Dick Klayman and Greg Gallo were correct. Two months doesn't make a season, and the Yankees lead over the Red Sox was just six games. Anybody with a history of pennant races involving the two clubs knows that is a very slim margin at a very early date in the schedule.

Still, before the first drop of Memorial Day beer flowed from the keg, I believed the Yankees had reduced the best division in baseball to a chase for second place, with the entire A.L. East choking on their fumes.

I was so sure of this that I wrote that the Yankees magic number was 112. That drew a few strange looks in the clubhouse, but nobody asked me what I was smoking either.

Of course, nobody within the organization admitted anything was over. But the way the Yankees went about their business against the Red Sox was the biggest example of why it was. After blowing a 4–0 lead in Friday night's loss, they rebounded with a 12–3 win Saturday. Sunday, they whipped the pitching-challenged Red Sox with seventeen hits and gave a struggling David Cone his weekly dose of much-needed run support.

"What we should do is concentrate on that it's still May and there is a long way to go," said Scott Brosius, who remained hot with a 3–for–4 day that included a solo homer and raised his average to .342. "The key for us is not to concentrate on who we are playing, but just playing well. When we play well, we have a good chance to win."

The first days of June the Yankees did nothing but win. They started the month at 37–13 and 7 1/2 games ahead of the Orioles in the A.L. East, and they didn't lose until June 11 at Montreal.

However, one night before that 7–5 defeat, they received a serious reminder that they weren't bulletproof, when Bernie Williams sprained his right knee on an awkward slide into third base during a 6–2 victory.

Was this the dagger to the heart of the Yankees? Could they survive an extended stretch of games without their best player? Who would replace Williams's .353 batting average and 45 RBIs in 59 games? Could

Chad Curtis, a .280 hitter playing regularly in left, hold up playing every day in center field?

When Williams suffered the injury, he didn't leave the game immediately, so it didn't appear that serious. He scored the Yankees final run on Brosius's single, and played center field for the home sixth. But Williams felt something wasn't right.

"It was stiffening up," reported Williams, who believed he caught a cleat in the moist dirt that caused the funky looking slide. "I thought I better ice it down before it gets any worse."

He was replaced by Curtis, and the way Williams limped while exiting Olympic Stadium told anybody who saw it that the All-Star center fielder was in great discomfort. Even though the Yankees were describing the injury as a mild sprain, trained eyes knew it was worse.

"It hurts right now, I have to wait and see," Williams said, the hinge supported by a heavy wrap. He winced when he pulled on his slacks. "Right now it's pretty painful."

He was examined by Dr. Stuart Hershon and underwent a battery of tests that included an MRI the next day in New York.

Williams's injury took the attention from the Yankees ninth straight victory and overshadowed Hideki Irabu's latest strong outing. In six-plus innings, Irabu allowed two runs and five hits. After serving up a monster homer to Rondell White to open the seventh, Irabu sat through a 36-minute rain delay and was done for the night.

"It's the best he has pitched the last few times out," Torre said of Irabu, who improved to 6–1. His 1.59 ERA and .183 batting average against were the best in the majors.

On top of the strong hurling, Irabu collected his first hit as a professional player, a line-drive single to center in the second. The single was the first hit by a Yankee pitcher since Larry Gowell doubled off the Brewers Jim Longborg on October 4, 1972. Irabu also provided a sacrifice bunt in a two-run fourth.

"I was surprised," he said of the hit. "When I swung the bat, the ball hit it."

In addition to putting a damper on Irabu's outing, Williams's injury took the shine off Paul O'Neill's three-hit game, which extended his hitting streak to a career-high seventeen games. Also glossed over was Tim Raines's 800th career stolen base, which he accomplished in the city where he started his career in 1979, as an Expo. Raines, fifth on the all-time stolen base list, is the fourth player in this century to reach 800 bags, and he received the base as a memento.

Losing a high-profile player to injury hadn't bothered the Yankees one iota. When Mariano Rivera went on the DL, Mike Stanton stepped into the closer's role and the Yankees went 11–2 without the All-Star reliever. They were without DH Chili Davis since the first week of the season. They went 5–1 when Martinez was out, and were 6–0 with Derek Jeter on the DL.

Still, there is a limit to how much covering up any team can do. And after a slow April, Williams carried a scorching May into June. His two hits in the game in which he was injured gave him 10 in 20 at-bats (.500) and raised his batting average to .353.

The next day, the severity of the injury forced the Yankees to place Williams on the DL for the third time in two years.

"He is going to need every bit of the two weeks," Joe

Torre said. "There's no clunker in there that needs surgery. It's a sprained knee and basically he will rest it. When he feels better, we'll rehab it."

To take Williams's roster spot, the Yankees called up outfielder Ricky Ledee from Columbus (Triple A).

"I'm not bringing him up to sit on the bench," Torre said of the twenty-four-year-old, left-handed hitting Ledee, who for the past three years has been regarded as the Yankees best prospect. "He will see action."

"It's kind of emotional for me right now," Ledee told the *Post* from Columbus thirty minutes after he received the big league call. "I've always dreamed of playing in the big leagues and getting that call. It's been a long time. This is my ninth season in the minors."

"He makes us all better," Curtis said of Williams. "I like center, but here I would rather play left. For however long I'm here, I want to play next to Bernie. It's a treat to play out there with him. I like to think I can cover left field like a center fielder, and that helps the team. I'm impressed with the way he goes about his job. He's one of the best players in the game, and the way he acts, you wouldn't know it."

Meanwhile, the Yankees prepared for their first meeting with the Indians, the team that sent them home from the A.L. Division Series last October with a terrible taste in their mouths.

Groggy from a cross-country flight from Seattle, where he attended a mundane meeting of baseball owners—is there any other kind of owners meeting?—Steinbrenner perked up when the conversation turned toward the Indians invading Yankee Stadium for the start of a three-game series between the A.L. East and Central leaders.

The hurt remained in Steinbrenner's gut. He will never forget Mariano Rivera feeding Sandy Alomar a home run pitch in Game 4 that turned the series around. That Cleveland is Steinbrenner's hometown, and the Indians are an organization with a state-of-the-art facility just like the one the Boss lusts for, makes his hurt deeper.

"We have a score to settle with them," he told the *Post*. "It has developed into a great rivalry because they are a great team and a great organization.

"It will be good for New York. The Indians have always been a tremendous competitor of the Yankees going back to the Bob Feller days," the Boss said. "It always came down to the Yankees and Indians for the A.L. title."

And last fall it went the Indians way.

"I don't forget those things, it sure hurts," the Boss said. "We couldn't get the last four outs. Their first baseman"—Jim Thome—"made a big play, and [Mariano] Rivera's inability to get the outs . . . those are tough things, but you have to get through them."

Playing without Williams was expected to take a little edge off the series with the Indians. Instead, rain washed out the first two games, and the Yankees, behind David Cone's seventh straight victory, won the finale 4–2, when Tino Martinez drove in three runs.

While Rivera said he had already downloaded the bitter memory from his mind, others still felt the sting.

"I remember the feeling, and it was not a good one," outfielder Chad Curtis said. "I haven't played the game forever, but I have played long enough to know that you don't play on a team with a chance to win it all that many times. I felt like it was an opportunity that slipped away, that something special slipped away."

On Tuesday, June 19, the Yankees started to get whole when Derek Jeter returned from the DL, where he was shelved with a strained rib-cage muscle.

With Williams out and a brutal schedule at hand, the Yankees were in the middle of what some believed to be their first real challenge of the season. Others thought that if they came through a seventeen-game stretch against Cleveland, Baltimore, Atlanta, and the Mets in good shape, it would be their last challenge.

After splitting a four-game series in Cleveland by losing the finale 11–0, when the Indians raked Hideki Irabu and Bartolo Colon limited them to three hits in eight innings, they were 4–4 with two games rained out.

Ahead was the toughest part of the slate due to four games with the Braves—two at Yankee Stadium and two in Atlanta—and three with the Mets at Shea Stadium, which was being billed as New York Baseball Armageddon II.

Thanks to spotless relief from Jeff Nelson, Mike Stanton, and Mariano Rivera, who posted his seventeenth save, and three hits by Chad Curtis and two RBIs from Tim Raines, the Yankees took a 6–4 win from the Braves on June 22.

While Greg Maddux wasn't the loser—Dennis Martinez was—the Yankees collected nine hits and scored three runs off the best pitcher in the game.

In his fourth major league start, Orlando "El Duque" Hernandez ran into his first taste of difficulty. After beating putrid Tampa Bay 7–1 in his major league debut on June 3, he toppled an equally inept Montreal club 11–1, a complete game four-hitter.

The muscular lineup of the Braves didn't chase Hernandez's sweeping curveball. They made the Cuban refugee come in with fastballs. And when El Duque has to do that, his pitches beg to be spanked.

El Duque lasted 3 2/3 innings, gave up six hits and walked four as the Braves took a 7–2 victory to Atlanta, where the teams would meet the next night.

Welcome to Atlanta. Read those words at the airport in late June and you better be prepared to sweat. A suffocating blanket of heat turned Turner Field into an outdoor sauna bath. As sweat dripped from every pore in the house, David Cone never let the Braves see him perspire.

Not after the light-hitting Ozzie Guillen hit Cone's fourth pitch over the right-field wall. Not after Andruw Jones's loud RBI double in the second inning. Not after Darryl Strawberry misplayed Javy Lopez's line drive to left in the fourth.

While everyone around Cone was drenched, he stayed cool. While Braves starter Kevin Millwood wilted, Cone remained collected.

"I like the heat," Cone said. "It helps an old guy get looser."

Cone dug the oppressive conditions so much that he went seven innings to beat the Braves 10–6 in front of a sold-out crowd of 48,980, and improve his record to 10–2.

"I would rather pitch in the heat than the cold," said the thirty-five-year-old Cone, who gave up three runs (two earned) and five hits. He hit one batter, didn't issue a walk, and fanned seven. Adding to the sparkling night, he also drove in a run with a fielder's choice ground ball in the four-run fourth.

Proving that the game-time temperature of 92 didn't affect him, Cone's best innings were the fifth, sixth, and seventh, when he retired nine of ten batters.

The victory, which included Paul O'Neill's ninth homer, Joe Girardi's three-hit, two-RBI night, and a two-hit, two-RBI performance from Tino Martinez, pushed the Yankees record to a staggering 52–19. It also hiked their A.L. East lead over the second-place Red Sox to ten games.

"Once we got the lead I was able to settle down," said Cone, who'd been rocked for five runs and eight hits—two homers—in his last start against the Indians, when he had a nine-game winning streak stopped. "My splitter saved me tonight. It was the first time I had a good one in the last three or four starts. I made an effort to go back to the hesitation in my delivery. I would rather not stop, but it helps me get back to my checkpoints."

At 10–2, Cone's name started to be linked to the All-Star team. While Torre said his veteran was deserving of a trip to Denver the following month, Cone hesitated.

"The rest would be nice," he said, referring to the three-day break non-All Stars enjoy.

And when the Yankees charter got them back to New York at four in the morning, Cone and his playmates could have used more time to rest before invading Shea.

Yankee Profile:
Paul O'Neill

Laughter is not a sound you usually hear when you watch Paul O'Neill burn white-hot on a baseball field. If watching O'Neill on television is your only avenue into the Yankees fiery right fielder, you rarely see the wide, toothy midwestern smile that he more often flashes off the field.

A classic rock fan whose hobby is playing the drums, O'Neill can be found sitting in front of his locker singing softly along to songs such as Meatloaf's "Paradise by the Dashboard Lights." Since one of Joe Torre's few rules is clubhouse music could not be played loudly, neither O'Neill nor Meatloaf can be heard very well. The only exception to the rule is on the days David Wells pitches. Wells, a heavy metal fan, will pump up his speakers to ear-blasting decibels as a way to help him get psyched up for a game. As for O'Neill, the only Meatloaf song that he has a problem with is, "Two Out of Three Ain't Bad."

For three hours a night, two out of three is unacceptable to O'Neill. A big leaguer since 1985, a professional ballplayer since 1981 and a kid raised on sports in Columbus, Ohio, O'Neill knows failure is part of sports landscape. That, however, doesn't mean he has to accept it. Three out of three is more like it. And if that results in a helmet slammed, an umpire yelled at, a water cooler assaulted, or O'Neill beating himself up in the runway behind the dugout, well, that's part of the gig. And who knows how many calls O'Neill's gotten from an ump who simply doesn't want to hear his complaints? More than one manager believes O'Neill has intimidated more than a few umps with his arguing. At thirty-five, O'Neill isn't going to change. On the field, that is. Away from the ballpark, he's as calm as they come.

"I used to watch SportsCenter just to watch him snap," said Rye Brook neighbor and first-year teammate Darren Holmes. "Then you see him do so many things with his kids around the house, and he isn't the same guy. The difference is amazing."

Back at the park, well, O'Neill has to have a fire burning hot in his belly. David Cone calls him the "John McEnroe of baseball." Yet, what's important to note—and teammates do it often—is this: once O'Neill lets the rage over making an out escape, there is no better teammate.

"I've been on teams where guys make an out, snap and then sulk," former infielder and current batting practice pitcher Dale Sveum says. "There is no sulking from him. He makes an out and gets mad. But if the next guy hits a homer, Paul is right there on the steps to shake his hand. I've seen other guys sit there and not do a thing."

It's not hard to find out where O'Neill picked up the intense desire to excel. You just have to return to the rural Ohio household headed by Charles O'Neill.

"I grew up with four older brothers, and competition between brothers is probably the strongest competition there is," O'Neill said. "We were always competing at every sport we played. Losing wasn't easy for any of us to take. I don't know, I guess it's the way you're wired."

There are times when he doesn't like what he sees from himself on television, but there isn't a whole lot he can do about it. He doesn't know if it helps or hurts him. What he simply knows is this: he has to care about what he's doing or he can't do it.

"We were taught by my dad that you play something to win and you play something well," said O'Neill, a high school quarterback and safety as well as star outfielder and basketball player.

O'Neill has come to know how to win. He has three World Series rings, hitting .471 for the 1990 Reds, and playing on one leg for the Yankees victory over the Braves in 1996. He's appeared in four straight postseasons with the Yankees and has been a major part of them winning the World Series two of the last three years.

You could say he was playing well too. Going into this season, when he posted a .317 average with 25 home runs and 116 RBIs, O'Neill was a .315 hitter in his five Yankee seasons and ranked fifth among all-time Yankee batting leaders with 500 games played. In that time his career batting average has moved from .259 to .290. And he's been an American League All-Star three times, and once in the N.L. Finally, he led the A.L. in hitting with a .359 average in the strike-shortened 1994 season.

Once there were just his brothers and himself. Now, there are three children who watch every muscle twitch of their dad. Now, he sees a lot of himself in the kids. Again, he doesn't know if it's good or bad.

"I see it in my kids and it's hard for me to correct them for it," O'Neill said. "My wife [Nevalee], she doesn't understand, she didn't grow up that way. I mean, I didn't tell my kids anything, it's just the way they are. I see it in sports. I don't think it has anything to do with personality. When they start playing something, whether it's baseball or Candyland, it usually ends up with one of them crying because they lost. I hate to see it but that's the way they are. [Nevalee] shakes her head at it and says, 'Look what you've done.'

"I don't push anything upon them as far as what they should do or what their interests are, but I can tell already that they like to compete."

And if the often cold world of sports, with all its heart-breaking moments, is where Andrew (eight), Aaron (five), and Alexandra (two) want to go, Pop isn't about to throw up a roadblock.

"I grew up with sports being my whole life," O'Neill explained. "I wouldn't want to do it any other way. When I look back to when I was little and what I went through with sports, they're all great memories. I would hope my kids have those same memories."

Meanwhile, Pop had prepared himself for another October war. His intensity and productive bat have moved O'Neill to the top of George Steinbrenner's list of favorites. There are some in the Yankees universe who believe that when he's finished—after next season—the Boss will recognize his contributions with a plaque in Monument Park. The snapshots are there: chasing down Luis Polonia's fly ball on one leg in Game 5 of the 1996 World Series to preserve a 1–0 win; somehow creating a slide into second to keep the Yankees alive in the ninth inning of last year's Game 5 against Cleveland in the riveting A.L. Division Series; hard line drives everywhere.

Watch him go at it with every pitch meaning something and you'll understand that O'Neill knows only one way: the way Charles taught him.

"Like I said, I don't know if it's good or bad. I've had people tell me I shouldn't take it so hard, and over the years sometimes I agree with them," O'Neill recalled. "But as soon as I don't care, I don't want to play anymore. It seems like when you're going through the motions, you're taking up a uniform somebody else should have."

On May 21, O'Neill decided he would wear the Yankees uniform for at least another year. In the summer of 1997 he had dropped a few hints that he was tiring of hearing T-ball results on the phone in a lonely hotel room. But the fire was still in his belly, and being part of the best team in baseball had the embers stoked.

When it was made, the marriage of O'Neill and the Yankees had plenty of doubters. An Ohio kid traded to New York who exchanges the tranquillity of Cincinnati for the Bronx Zoo. Surely, it sounded like the beginning of a disaster. Nevalee cried when she heard the news.

Six years later the union is as strong as there is in sports.

"I'm happy to be here and I don't see a need to be anywhere else," O'Neill said. "My family is happy here. Right now this is where I want to be."

Both sides agreed it will last at least through the 1999 season, when O'Neill and the team he has come to love agreed to a one-year extension. Currently in the final year of a four-year deal that paid him $4.9 million in 1998, the extension calls for a $250,000 signing bonus and $6.25 million next season. The Yankees hold an option for the year 2000 at $6.5 million. Never consumed by money, O'Neill only asked that the Yankees be fair with him. The rest he left up to his agent, Joe Bick.

"An agent's job is to take what you want and to run with it," he said.

Bick didn't have to run very hard or break a sweat. In October 1994, after the strike-shortened season when O'Neill led the A.L. with a .359 average, it took all of forty-five minutes to negotiate a four-year pact. This one took a little longer, but not once did it get ugly, like so many other contract talks always seem to do.

"Paul and his representative both know what we wanted, which is each other," GM Brian Cashman said. "It's always tougher to do things during the season because there are so many other things going on. But Paul is an important piece now and in the future.

"He means so much to this place," Cashman added of O'Neill, who arrived after the 1992 season in exchange for Roberto Kelly and what now ranks as former GM Gene Michael's biggest heist. "A lot of our success started when he got here, and I can't say enough about him. We both made a commitment to each other. He's family, and I'm glad it will continue."

Even though O'Neill will be thirty-six when next season starts, he could have conceivably landed a more lucrative deal from another team had he tested the free agent waters. But leaving was never an option to O'Neill.

"It was a very simple decision for me, an easy thing for me to do," he explained. "There are a lot of positives to playing here. Everybody talks about New York and the pressures, but there's pressure everywhere. If you play well, they like you. If you don't, they hate you. There may be more people here, that's all."

As for not trying to extract another guaranteed year from the Yankees, who really have no long-range replacement for him in their system, O'Neill is comfortable with the option language:

"I will take it year by year. If I continue to play, it will be in New York. That's what I wanted and what they wanted."

Now they have each other at least until the end of next season. However, with the way they admire each other, and O'Neill not showing any sign of slowing up, it's almost a lock that the option year will be picked up and O'Neill will finish the first baseball season of the next century in pinstripes.

"This is as much fun as I've had playing baseball," said O'Neill, who has World Series rings from the 1996 and 1998 Yankees and the 1990 Reds. "I don't think there's any reason to change."

Certainly not on the field. Even in the most pedestrian game, O'Neill can liven things up in the dugout. Watching him make an out on television is okay because his bat, helmet, or hands can't penetrate your screen. But sit in the Yankee dugout and it's a different story.

Because they're thrill-seekers at heart, O'Neill's teammates anticipate the latest snap. Nobody disappears into the tunnel for an O'Neill at-bat. It's not that they just want to see the reaction to failure—in fact, O'Neill hitting in the clutch is one of baseball's treasured moments. However, when he doesn't come through, they get a rush off the emotion. Often his teammates have to hold laughter for fear of getting caught breaking up as he screams at himself.

He cares about wearing the most famous uniform in sports. He cares about his four at-bats a night. He doesn't care how much money he makes, because he can't spend what he has. Most of all, O'Neill appreciates what playing for the Yankees means.

"I've stood where Babe Ruth stood, I met Mickey Mantle, I've played with Don Mattingly," O'Neill told the audience at the New York Baseball Writers' Dinner. "I'd say it's turned out all right."

For him and the club.

7

Baseball Armageddon: Yankees vs. Mets

Interleague play was the brainstorm of the owners, who, as is always their practice, were looking for a quick fix after the game was shut down and the World Series was cancelled in 1994 by the work stoppage. Instead of learning a lesson and letting the greatest game in the world heal itself, the owners believed a gimmick would help.

Bill Giles, then the president of the Phillies, pushed the idea, saying that Philadelphia fans should have the chance to see Ken Griffey, Jr. play in a regular season game at Veterans Stadium. Of course, what Giles conveniently forgot to tell people when he was selling his plan was that interleague play was going to pit teams from matching divisions. For example, the N.L. East would play the A.L. East, the N.L. Central would wrestle the A.L. Central, and the N.L. West would tangle with the A.L. West. Thus, Griffey was never going to play in the Vet during the regular season.

And what baseball fans were left with were yawns such as the Tigers-Astros and Phillies-Blue Jays. Yet the owners occasionally luck out. And the Mets-Yankees match-up was just that. For the New York baseball fan, three days in the end of June in Queens was heaven.

Still smarting from losing two of three in 1997, the Mets were a much-improved club. Say what you will about Bobby Valentine—and plenty always seems to be said—he had the Mets playing over their heads. This time, it was at Shea Stadium, a venue some think has outlived its usefulness. Despite an interesting team to watch, fans stay away. Maybe they didn't believe the Mets would be in the hunt for a postseason spot down to the wire? Maybe New York has been spoiled by stars, most of whom play for the Yankees? And possibly, the Shea experience isn't what it used to be.

However, for three nights at the end of June the place was electric. Nobody complained about the jets torching the sky with noise on their way in and out of LaGuardia Airport. And for one player, Shea's warts were easily ignored.

Because Darryl Strawberry broke in for the Mets, led them to the 1986 World Championship, and developed into one of the biggest names in New York baseball history and was now a Yankee, *Post* sports editor Greg Gallo believed Strawberry would be the perfect man to write a diary for the paper. On the other side, Gallo got Al Leiter, who had played with the Yankees and was now the Mets ace.

*Here is what Strawberry wrote going into the Subway Series:

Great memories, that's what I think about when somebody brings up Shea Stadium. The memories I have of Shea Stadium are of the fans. We got 40,000 a night. They supported us as a team and as a player and that made you go out and perform at your best . . .

I remember the first day I walked in there as a player, it was pretty exciting. I had just turned 21 and was pretty nervous that the time finally came that I was going to be with the ballclub. We weren't a very good ballclub when I came up there but that was the turning point as far as the changes for that organization . . . I was the first one to really come up that was going to be an everyday player that they had drafted and brought through the minor league system. From that point, we started playing a lot more younger players.

It doesn't seem like that was 15 years ago. Every time I ride by that ballpark or fly over it, I always look over there because that's a place I can never forget. I can never forget the years there that were so successful.

I am with the Yankees now but I hope I am not treated as the enemy because there were a lot of treats there, for myself and the fans. We got the opportunity to put that team on the map and we did. That's something I can always say I am proud of, that we started at the bottom and climbed to the top . . .

Mets-Yankees at Shea will probably be crazy. Each team is fighting for the town of New York, you know, who is the best and all that stuff. Over the last couple of years the Yankees have established themselves as the best one in New York.

Having played the Angels at Shea Stadium when Yankee Stadium was closed was a big plus for us . . . because most of the guys had never been there before. We saw what it was like but it's going to be a totally different atmosphere this time around when we go over there to play.

To me, what I remember about the last time was that I still recognized a lot of the people that worked there. People came up to me and they were real happy to see me. A lot of people who work there saw a lot of great things out of me playing in that ballpark. It's New York and it's something that you just don't forget.

Winning the World Series in 1986 was the best and leaving was the worst. That's something I will probably regret for a long time, leaving there. But at the same time, I mean, it wasn't a contract situation. I was more upset that we were giving everybody away. Once Lenny Dykstra had left, I pretty much set my sights on departing, too. Lenny was one of my favorites and one of the guys I knew was going to be able to help us if he got the opportunity to play every day.

• • •

One player who wouldn't be involved in the series was right-handed reliever Jeff Nelson. The Yankees placed him on the fifteen-day DL and recalled right-hander Mike Buddie from Columbus (Triple A) before Game 1.

Nelson had been suffering from lower back pain for two weeks, officially described as strain and a pinched nerve. Later, it would be diagnosed as a bulging disc.

"It's the safest thing to do with a reliever," Joe Torre said. "It's safe for everybody. And with the All-Star break, it gives us a few extra days."

"I am not happy, especially playing the Mets and wanting to get into the series," Nelson said, "but I want to get it over with."

For Game 1 of the Subway Series, the Mets started the left-handed Leiter against Hideki Irabu. Home runs by Brian McRae and Edgardo Alfonzo in the fifth inning staked the Mets to a 3–1 lead and got the Shea crowd of 53,404 stoked. Scott Brosius, probably the biggest surprise of the Yankee season, tied the score 3–3 with an RBI single in the sixth. After Leiter hurt his left knee covering first base, Bobby Valentine brought in righty Mel Rojas to face Paul O'Neill with two runners on base. After O'Neill hit a three-run homer to left-center on Rojas's first pitch, a controversy was born.

Why did Valentine bring in Rojas, a bust since joining the Mets in 1997, to face O'Neill? Where was lefty Dennis Cook? Valentine pointed out that O'Neill hits lefties as well as righties. Still, he took incredible heat from every second-guessing media outlet following the Yankees 8–4 victory.

In Game 2, backed by a three-run homer by Tino Martinez in the fourth inning and a solid 6 1/3 innings of pitching from Andy Pettitte, the Yankees rolled to a 7–3 victory. In the seventh, Valentine summoned lefty Bill Pulsipher to face O'Neill. Prior to the game Valentine got into a discussion with a fan behind the Met dugout over his decision to bring in Rojas. Now, a nanosecond after O'Neill laced an RBI single to right to drive in the fourth and final run of the inning, Valentine emerged from the dugout.

He glanced up at the press box as if to say, "See, O'Neill hits left-handers too."

Later, Valentine said he was looking for family members in the seats, but no one in the press bought it, and brought even more pressure to bear on the Mets manager. Post columnist Wallace Mathews labeled Valentine "Captain Queeg" and took Valentine to task. While Valentine basked in the attention, even if it was negative, the Yankees kept a low profile.

Game 3 developed into a nose-to-nose pitching duel featuring Masato Yoshi and Orlando "El Duque" Hernandez. The biggest melting pot in the world—New York—was serving up an international pitching gem.

Carlos Baerga gave the Mets a 1–0 lead in the sixth and Scott Brosius tied the score 1–1 in the seventh with a homer. Luis Lopez's sacrifice fly to right field scored Baerga with the game-winning run in the home ninth, but not before some huge controversy erupted.

Paul O'Neill caught the ball going into the right center-field gap and flung it back to the infield where Brian McRae was foolishly dancing off first. O'Neill's throw went to Derek Jeter and then to Tino Martinez, who bobbled the ball as he crossed the bag trying to double off McRae. Baerga, meanwhile, scored from third. There was some confusion among the fans, the players—including Jeter and Martinez—and, yes, even among those in the press box, as few realized that as soon as Baerga dented the plate, what happened to McRae made no difference. Still, the Mets took the last game of the Subway Series.

A notable absence at the series was George Steinbrenner. In order to be on hand for his grandson George Michael's second birthday and to watch three granddaughters compete in an important swim meet, the Boss watched the Subway Series from his Tampa headquarters.

"I am very proud of our team," the Boss said. "First, we had four tough games with Atlanta, the number one team in the National League, and won three of four from them. Then we took an airplane from Atlanta home late in the morning, and the Mets had been playing the Orioles in New York so they were ready and rested. And the Mets did a helluva job hyping the series, but our kids took two of three. The third one had a little controversy, but that's the way it goes."

And while he liked what he saw, he was glad to be done with the Mets.

"It was a great series and the Mets did a nice job. There were a few things I would have done differently, but they did a nice job," the Boss said. "But I wouldn't want to see it more than one time a year. It overshadows our rivalries with Boston, Baltimore, and Cleveland."

Along with the rest of the Yankee brass, GM Brian Cashman agreed it was very nice having the Mets out of the way.

"I'm happy it's over with," Cashman said. "All games count the same. The series against Detroit counts the same as the series against the Mets."

The Yankees then hosted the resurging Phillies for a three-game series. By now the lead over the Red Sox was ten furlongs and everything was perfect in the Yankees world. Yet, the Bombers hadn't forgotten how the Phillies reacted in 1997 when they swept a three-game Labor Day series at the Vet. Many Phillies admitted it was their playoffs, and they acted that way, celebrating after each victory. Watching perhaps the worst team in baseball behave this way stuck with the Yankee players.

"Where are they going after the season is over?" one player asked. "I didn't know the playoffs started the first day of September."

It was easy to see the Yankees were focused from the start. They scored four runs off rookie Carlton Loewer in the second when Darryl Strawberry led off with a homer. Five more runs in the fifth put the game away. Meanwhile, David Cone blew the Phillies away, going the distance to win his seventh straight.

More of the same followed the next night, the first

day of July, when David Wells allowed two runs (one earned) and seven hits to post a 5–2 victory.

Because Phillies manager Terry Francona wanted to give Curt Schilling an extra day's rest, the premier strike-out pitcher in the National League, and one who'd dominated the Yankees a year before, wasn't going to pitch Thursday night. Instead, he would go against the Expos on Friday. Was Schilling ducking the best team in baseball? More than a few people around the Phillies believed that was the case. Many Yankees were disappointed at not getting a shot at one of the best chuckers in the game.

Five runs off Hideki Irabu in three-plus innings gave the Phillies a 5–0 lead after 4 1/2 innings on that Thursday, but Paul O'Neill hit a two-run homer in the three-run eighth and Tino Martinez sent the game into extra innings with a two-out, three-run bomb off Mark Leiter in the ninth.

"It was a fastball middle in," said Martinez, who upped his season home run total to fourteen. "He has a pretty decent sinker. It was a mistake pitch I think."

Until now, Leiter had filled in very well as the Phillies closer with Ricky Bottalico battling elbow problems. However, his pitch selection in the fatal ninth turned a few heads.

"It was a sinker that didn't sink," Leiter said. "It sank in the upper deck. Two outs and nobody on. That's not disappointing, that's embarrassing."

Ricky Ledee went on to win it with a single in the eleventh.

"I'm happy to say that nothing this club does surprises me," Joe Torre said. "They don't back off. This was some kind of comeback, obviously."

The victory gave the Yankees a three-game winning streak, which swelled to ten after the All-Star break, when the Yankees took four straight in St. Petersburg against the Devil Rays.

With three months to go, the A.L. East race was over. Everybody knew it.

Everyone but the man who signed the checks, that is.

Steinbrenner may have been raised in Cleveland, but he never wanted to be a big fish in a small pond. Even if the pond is New York City. No, the Boss has always measured his Yankees against a bigger backdrop than Manhattan, Queens, Brooklyn, Staten Island, and the Bronx.

"We haven't won anything yet," he said from Tampa the day after the Subway Series was complete. "We won the bragging rights to the city for the second time in a row, whatever that means. But we haven't won anything yet."

8

Bernie's Knee and Dave's Foot

"**W**e haven't won a thing yet" became the Yankee mantra. The players said it as often as they said hello to each other. Let everybody else talk about the Yankees chances of breaking the 1906 Cubs record of 116 victories or the A.L. mark of 111 set by the 1954 Indians, the team Steinbrenner grew up adoring. All that jazz about whether David Wells, David Cone, or Andy Pettitte were worthy of a Cy Young was outside noise.

Privately, however, the Yankees felt real good about themselves, for they'd been winning despite the loss of designated hitter Chili Davis, and they'd done without Bernie Williams. What's more, none of the eight position players were in the midst of a career year, and the bridge between starters and closer Mariano Rivera had been missing a plank or two. It was starting pitching, the biggest question mark in March, that had been the vehicle the Yankees had driven to the top.

"It all comes down to pitching, and we have done that very well," Torre observed. "It doesn't surprise me that we've played this well. I am a little surprised by the record. Even though you play well, it doesn't mean you're going to win all the games."

When he wasn't sitting on top of the pinstriped horse, imploring it to improve its position, the Boss understood why his high-priced collection of talent had the baseball world buzzing.

"Joe Torre has a feel for it and he is doing a tremendous job," Steinbrenner said.

Torre certainly had. He handled what could have been touchy situations platooning players in left field and behind the plate with aplomb. But there was more work to do. Before the Yankees completed a West Coast swing early in August, Torre would have to find a spot for Davis's high-priced, switch-hitting bat in the lineup. That figured to take at-bats away from Tim Raines and Darryl Strawberry, both of whom contributed heavily to the wonderful first half.

While David Wells, the A.L. starting pitcher in the All-Star game, led a contingent of four Yankees to Denver for the game, and Bernie Williams, the other Yankee All-Star, was in Tampa working on his sprained right knee, Brian Cashman was relaxing at his Connecticut home. The GM's team was eleven lengths up and there were no games slated from July 6 through 8.

Then the cell phone rang. Playing for Tampa (Single A) in Clearwater at Jack Russell Stadium, Williams had reinjured his sprained right knee five innings into the first game of the rehabilitation assignment and had to be removed. In center field, Williams experienced discomfort after a throw to third base. The Yankees had survived nicely without their best all-around player. However, there is a limit to how much any team can do without its cleanup hitter and center fielder. Suddenly, the air of calm around the Yankees bubble was pierced.

Cashman didn't need to understand the exact words Williams was saying via a car phone on the twenty-minute trip from Clearwater to Tampa to know that the player was depressed.

"I had trouble hearing him speak, he was down," the subdued GM said. "He was bummed out.

"It was a routine play, he didn't step in a hole or anything. It's a setback, but the doctor doesn't think it's a major setback. [Williams] heard no pop, and there was no inflammation. It could simply be scar tissue."

After conferring with Dr. Allan Miller, who examined Williams in Tampa, Cashman explained, "He didn't say it was another sprain. We thought three weeks when it happened, but sometimes it takes four to six. The doctor said this was the knee telling us it needed more time. It wasn't that the knee wasn't responding, it just has to slow down a bit."

When the Yankees arrived at the Tampa Bay Devil Ray stadium, Tropicana Field, for a Thursday afternoon workout called by Torre, they found Williams anxious to meet them. Yes, he was down about not being healthy enough to be activated, but he'd learned from experience that unless a leg injury is completely healed, there's no sense rushing back.

"The next day [Tuesday], it felt better. Wednesday it felt even better, and today I am right at the point where I was when I started playing," said Williams, who was leading the A.L. with a .353 average at the break.

Williams believed he could start taking batting practice immediately, but the Yankees were approaching the situation with baby steps. Their plan called for him to start another minor league rehabilitation assignment about a week later.

"Bernie wants to hit but I told him we can't let him do that until the doctor allows him to hit," Torre said.

If you didn't know Williams, your first thought would be that he was bothered by missing an extended period of time in his free agent walk year. Surely, the longer he sat out, the more money it would cost him. And then there was the usual paranoia that surrounds the Yankees.

Were they taking it extra slow with Williams in order to drive his free agent price down, at Steinbrenner's request? At first blush that sounded ridiculous. However, with the shenanigans that have gone on in the past around this team, nothing is ever completely out of the question.

"This is very disappointing, are you kidding me," said Williams, who underwent an MRI that showed no structural damage to the knee. "I was hopeful of playing here."

Since the discomfort he'd felt had been due to scar tissue breaking up, Williams believed the knee was sending him a message. "All that means is that the knee wasn't ready to start playing yet."

He didn't know when that time would arrive, but until he felt perfect, he wasn't going to try.

"I'm going to make sure when I go out there I'm a hundred percent," Williams said. "The only thing I have to make sure I can do is push off and throw. That will tell me I can play."

Meanwhile, the *Post* learned that the Yankees had made contact with the Angels regarding a possible deal involving Darrin Erstad, a twenty-four-year-old superstar in the making. Was there any end to George Steinbrenner's people trying to get better? Here was the best team assembled in possibly twenty years, yet there was still talk about adding another player to improve it.

Say what you want about Steinbrenner, but his thirst for being the best has rubbed off on his employees. And it wasn't just about this year. Everyone around the Yankees knew there was a big chance Bernie Williams might leave as a free agent. So the inquiry was made with an eye to next year. While GM Brian Cashman didn't say who made the contact or when it was made, he didn't deny a deal involving Erstad was discussed with the Angels.

"I have always told our scouts to be aggressive and stir things up," Cashman said. "It makes me happy that they are out there talking to people. That means we are working and hammering away."

That's also the reason they monitored Cardinal center fielder Brian Jordan across the second half of the season, in the event he doesn't resign with St. Louis and becomes a free agent. The Cardinals have started talking with Jordan, but it's believed they won't have the money to bring him back after investing heavily in outfielder J.D. Drew.

The Angels acted the way you would expect since Erstad is the type of player franchises are built around.

"I asked them if George [Steinbrenner] had enough money to buy Disney," the Angels source said of the parent company that owns the California team.

Meanwhile, Jeff Nelson fractured a toe on his right foot when he walked into a coffee table in a St. Petersburg hotel room. Nelson was about to embark on an injury rehabilitation assignment for Tampa.

Suddenly, on a night when they were off, the Yankees suffered injuries to a pair of key performers. Was this the payback for all the wonderful things they'd experienced during the first half of the season?

As Williams and Nelson recovered, the Yankees took to

Tropicana Field trying to win their third straight against the Devil Rays, and it turned out to be the smoothest 2–0 victory seen in a while until Mariano Rivera raised the anxiety level in the ninth. But with runners on first and third and one out, Rivera induced Dave Martinez to ground back to the mound, and then he caught pinch-hitter Bobby Smith looking to end the game.

Cone improved to 13–2 and Rivera posted his twenty-fourth save.

The following game, something seemed askew when David Wells walked Quinton McCracken on four pitches with one out in the first inning. Wells hadn't walked anybody in his previous four starts, and only sixteen in 112 2/3 innings for the season. Three and a half hours later, after Wells lasted only five innings and walked three, the reason for his lack of control was discovered: an injured toe following a spill down a Palm Harbor staircase.

Wells knew he'd had enough after covering first base on Aaron Ledesma's grounder to Tino Martinez leading off the fifth. Following the close play, Wells fanned Mike DiFelice, gave up a homer to Miguel Cairo, the ninth hitter on the worst hitting team in the A.L., and retired Randy Winn on a fly to the warning track in left.

"It was fine, I took it easy the other day," said Wells, who suffered the injury three days earlier. X rays the same day were negative. "But the angle I hit the bag, it flared up. It was time to come out because overcompensating can lead to other things."

"We knew he had a problem going in," Torre said of Wells, who allowed one run, four hits, and had his string of 36 walkless innings stopped. Wells left the game leading 2–1. "When I saw him cover first base, I knew he was hurting a bit."

The victory upped the Bombers record to a staggering 65–20 and provided them with a fifteen-game bulge over the fading Red Sox in the A.L. East.

As for Wells, he didn't anticipate missing his next start in Toronto.

"I should be fine. I'll take it easy for the next few days and elevate it," he said. "It's very irritating when you can't go out and pitch."

But by Friday, five days later, Wells's toe problem wasn't well enough for him to pitch, and Ramiro Mendoza started a game Roger Clemens and the Blue Jays won 9–6.

Wells didn't take the ball until Monday, July 20, in the first game of a doubleheader against the Tigers at Yankee Stadium. It was a game that the Yankees lost 4–3 in seventeen innings, leaving 22 runners on base. And a game that reminded Joe Torre just what type of character his club had.

After thirty minutes to reenergize their minds with whatever methods they employed, Torre recognized more than one pissed off face in the dugout as the second game was set to start at 10:32.

"Everybody wanted to play," Torre said. "El Duque came down into the dugout with his spikes in his hand and told us he was ready. It was nice to see."

So too was a 4–3 victory that went to Hideki Irabu and raised his record to 9–3.

On Friday, July 24, the Yankees took a 5–4 decision from the White Sox in front of 44,264, and did it without having a batter hit with a runner in scoring position.

Still, the team was a little beat up. And on Monday they flew to California for their second, and final, West Coast trip, one that would have a heavy emphasis on doings off-the-field instead of on it.

Yankee Profile:
Bernie Williams

From the moment his fly ball landed in Brian Giles's glove to end the Yankee season in Game 5 of the 1997 A.L. Division Series in Jacobs Field, Bernie Williams's contract status took over center stage in the Yankees universe. He was the team's best player, a homegrown product and the player every financial decision in the organization revolved around. If you heard it once, you heard it a million times: "We have to save some money for Bernie."

However, Williams's performance in the division series was disappointing. He was 2–for–17 (.118), leading many in the organization to believe that he'd put pressure on himself to justify his desire for a multiyear contract for many millions, and that had an adverse affect on his play. Had he raked the Indians pitching, the Yankees would have had a hard time saying he wasn't worth top dollar. But having underachieved, the organization could argue, from the numbers, that Williams couldn't help the team to the next level.

After the Indians loss, Williams sat in a moribund Yankees clubhouse. Watching him, it was apparent the failure had cut very deep into what is one of the largest hearts in sports. After fifteen minutes, signs of life began to return as players moved toward the showers and started to pack for the brief but painful flight home. Not Bernie Williams. He remained sitting, half dressed, looking down into the carpet. Teammates stopped by to offer encouragement, and Williams met them with an empty stare and a simple nod. Eventually, he drifted off to the shower, and then dressed.

When it was finally time to go, Williams scribbled a check for the clubhouse attendant, shook his hand, and walked very slowly to the bus that would take the Yankees to the airport. If there was another Yankee taking the loss as hard as Williams, he wasn't in the room.

Almost before the plane landed, Williams's future in pin-stripes was the No. 1 topic in New York. Of course, he couldn't leave via free agency since he belonged to the Yankees for one more year. But unless the Yankees and agent Scott Boras closed a lot of ground in a hurry, Williams was headed to the arbitration table.

With talks going nowhere, former GM Bob Watson discussed a deal with his Detroit counterpart, Randy Smith. The talks reached the point where Smith thought he had a deal that would ship two of the Tigers top prospects to the Yankees for Williams. Once again Watson had the misimpression that he was running the Yankees. When he ran the deal by Steinbrenner and the Boss went to his "Baseball People," Watson was almost run out of town. Meanwhile, Smith was livid, accusing the Yankees of backing out on a deal.

Of course, Williams wasn't dealt. And when agent Boras's January 19, 1998, deadline for a contract to be reached had come and gone, Williams was headed back to the arbitration table. The Yankees were reluctant to meet Boras's wishes for $11 million a year for seven years. Boras privately chuckled at Watson saying the Bombers were proud to offer Williams $35 million for five years. When Steinbrenner pointed out that Williams, the Yankees best all-around player, was not in the class of, say, a Ken Griffey Jr., Boras countered that Williams's true value was linked to market value, not to other players who had signed long-term deals in previous years.

Meanwhile, Williams put his body through torturous workouts in Puerto Rico, where he kept a very low profile. He'd hired Boras, one of the most adept negotiators in the business, not only to handle his contract, but to deal with the flood of media requests.

"Bernie would rather not talk about it because nothing is happening," Boras said all winter. "Eventually, I will do what Bernie wants."

In the days leading to the February 18 arbitration hearing in Phoenix, it was assumed by everybody that it would go to the mat. However, in a stunning development, the case was settled for $8.25 million. Williams had filed for $9 million and the Yankees offered $7.5 million, so they met in the middle.

"This was a tough decision to make because we knew we were going to win," GM Brian Cashman said. "But based on the fact that Bernie is such a special person, we want to win this year and we really do want to keep him, we went ahead and did it."

The settlement was Cashman's first big project, and, according to him, George Steinbrenner left it in the neophyte GM's lap.

"I had to talk to George about it, to see if he would sign off," Cashman said. "He said, 'If you want to take the payroll to that level, you have my blessing.' He made it clear that it was my decision."

The $8.25 represented a $3 million raise for Williams. He was paid $5.25 million in 1997, when he copped his initial Gold Glove award and made the All-Star team for the first time. Williams hit .328 with 21 homers and 100 RBIs. The contract put him in a tie for fourteenth place on baseball's salary list in terms of annual average value, with Roger Clemens and Andres Galarraga. It also included a $50,000 bonus Williams earned for making the All-Star team. It was the second-highest one-year deal in history, falling short of the $8.5 million extension the Blue Jays gave Pat Hentgen after he won the 1996 Cy Young Award.

As Williams walked from Delta Flight 2140 to the elevator that would take him to the luggage carousel on the first floor of the Tampa Airport on February 18, 1998, the best baseball player in New York uttered the sweetest music a Yankee fan wanted to hear.

"Enough of this contract negotiation nonsense," Williams told the *Post*. "Let's play ball."

Following a winter spent in baseball's financial spotlight, the heart and soul of the Bombers was ready to sweat alongside Paul O'Neill, Tino Martinez, Chuck Knoblauch, and Chili Davis when he joined the second full-squad workout at Legends Field on February 20.

What he wasn't prepared to do was talk about a long-term contract with anybody. Not the *Post*. Not GM Brian Cashman. Not George Steinbrenner. A fractured relationship may have been put back together a tiny bit by avoiding an arbitration hearing Wednesday, but that was it. For far too long Williams was tired of fighting the Boss for every last nickel. Now one season away from free agency, Williams was going to play the season out and see what type of dollars were out there.

"I have had enough contracts for one year. I'm just going to concentrate on helping the team win, have a good year, and go from there."

While the arbitration process didn't sour Williams on New York, he wasn't ready to eliminate the other twenty-nine teams from his future.

"It's the only place I've played, so I certainly have emotions about that, but I have to think about other things," Williams said. "Now I can go play, which is the part I liked the most."

To classify Williams's start as slow would have been wrong. On May 10 he was hitting .303 but hadn't homered in 119 at-bats and had driven in just twelve runs in 31 games. But by the end of the month he'd jacked his average up to .352, had seven homers, 37 RBIs, and was named the A.L. Player of the Month. By the middle of June, Williams appeared to be on his way to a monster season. Then an awkward slide into third base in Montreal on June 10 placed him on the DL until July 18 with a sprained right knee. He was named to the All-Star team but couldn't play due to the injury. Ultimately, Williams went on to win a batting title, hitting .339 with 26 homers and driving in 97 runs in 128 games.

Under the intense spotlight of New York media, Williams managed to thrive and keep his dignity. He did admit that there had been moments during the magical Yankee season when his uncertain future had seeped into the most analytical mind in baseball.

What would happen after the season was over? Am I going to stay a Yankee? Or am I going to leave the only organization I have been associated with since the summer of 1986? And if I leave, where will I land?

Then, as quickly as those questions danced into his head, Williams worked hard to flush them. He made a promise to himself in March that the "Situation" wasn't going to interfere with what he expected to be a spectacular year for the Bombers and himself.

"When they came, I would immediately try to do something else," Williams said. "What I thought about is the type of season we're having and the type of year I'm having."

With one week left in the regular season, the Yankees were headed to the playoffs for the fourth straight season, so there were other games to be played. Yet, there was the real possibility that it could be the final week of Williams's regular season career as a Yankee.

"I haven't thought about that," Williams said at the time. "Whatever happens, it will be fine. The only thing I've tried to concentrate on is to have a decent year. For the most part I have accomplished that. A lot of pieces had to fall in place, and they have. Now I'm looking forward to playing in the postseason because you never take that for granted."

Regardless, it now appears Williams will get $12 million a season, as opposed to the $11 million per he was asking for before and the $7 million per the Yankees were offering. The Rangers, Rockies, and Dodgers were considered the front runners if he made the painful split from the Bronx. According to George Steinbrenner, the Yankees will do everything in their power to keep their best player.

"We will do our darndest," the Boss said. But would it be too little, too late?

Williams gives off an air of sincerity when he tells you he doesn't have a clue how the upcoming high-stakes negotiations will turn out. He listens when told it would be best for both parties for him to stay. But whether he stays or goes, the season would never be flushed from his memory bank.

"Regardless of what happens next year, I will never forget what this team has accomplished this year and that I was a part of it. We have a chance to be the best team in A.L. history and the best team in Yankees history," he said. "Considering all the great Yankee teams, that's saying something. I am proud to be part of it."

If September 27 was Bernie Williams's final regular season game in Yankee pinstripes, he picked a marvelous way to say adios to the Bronx.

Thanks to a 2-for-2 afternoon that included a sacrifice fly in an 8–3 Yankees victory over the Devil Rays at Yankee Stadium, the switch-hitting center fielder copped his first A.L. batting title. Williams's .339 edged out Red Sox first baseman Mo Vaughn, who finished at .337 after going 2–for–4. Torre pulled Williams in the sixth inning after learning from the press box that Vaughn couldn't catch him.

And what did Bernie Williams do? He jumped into weight-lifting clothes and headed for the workout room. But when David Wells entered the clubhouse, the workout was stalled because the crowd of 49,608 was calling for Williams.

"Boomer told me they weren't going to start the game until I went out there," Williams said. So he popped out of the dugout to give the throng several waves and a thumbs-up salute.

Williams is the eighth Yankee to lead the league in hitting, and the first since Paul O'Neill did it the strike-shortened 1994 season when he batted .359. Joe DiMaggio is the only Bomber to top the league twice. The Yankee Clipper did it in 1939 and 1940.

"It felt great," said Williams. "It's such a great feeling to add your name to the list of players who have accomplished that."

In addition to DiMaggio and O'Neill, Williams joins Babe Ruth, Lou Gehrig, Snuffy Stirnweiss, Mickey Mantle, and Don Mattingly, who led the A.L. in hitting as Yankees.

"I think there was more pressure on me to perform this year than any other year," Williams said. "Baseball is all about pressure and how you handle it. If you play here, you have to face adversity and different challenges. If you want to play here, you have to handle that. I take pride in that I played hard, and the fans appreciate that. I didn't know what was going to happen, but I knew that if I did my best on a daily basis, they would appreciate it."

No doubt they did appreciate it. Now the question was would the Boss. But the feeling in the clubhouse was that the Yankees were going to need a major upset to keep Williams in pinstripes.

9

The Big Pinstriped Unit?

The tail end of July means many things to many baseball teams. Some are hopelessly dead, delegated to another year of counting the days until the season ends so they can go about fooling their fans into believing next year will be different. Of course, it's never different for the Philadelphias, Milwaukees, and Montreals. They lie all winter and lose all summer.

For others, the final days of July brings excitement to the ballpark. Teams that have survived the first four months of the season are in a position to either win their division or cop a wild card spot. Suddenly, pennant races take shape, and fans who have had casual interest suddenly become experts.

However, there is a common denominator to the final week of July for both the also-rans and those clubs battling for a chance to play in October: July 31.

In order for a team to acquire a player without that player going through waivers, the deal has to be done before August 1. That makes July's final weeks a seven-day nightmare for GMs. For Brian Cashman it was triple the nightmare because the Yankees GM not only has to worry about his club, he must be constantly aware of what other clubs are doing just in case George Steinbrenner is curious about what the Indians are thinking.

Inside the Yankees universe, people clearly remembered the year before, when former GM Bob Watson was reprimanded by the Boss when Baltimore, the Yankees chief A.L. East opponent, acquired the veteran right-handed hitter Geronimo Berroa from Oakland. At the time, the Yankees were searching the baseball galaxy for a right-handed bat, but their asking price was, as usual, considerably higher than that of other teams, and Watson wasn't high on Berroa anyway.

This year, as the waiver deadline approached, the Bombers had a fifteen game lead over the Red Sox in the A.L. East and seemingly no needs on July 28, as they checked into Edison Field in Anaheim to open a West Coast trip. Their pitching was fine and they were expecting to get Chili Davis back from the DL in two weeks.

But nothing is ever as it seems with the Yankees. Since Randy Johnson was on the block—even if the confused Mariners said he wasn't—Cashman had to monitor the phones. No, there wasn't a burning need for the fireballing left-hander who had worn out his welcome in Seattle by quitting in the middle of the year, because the Mariners hadn't committed themselves to a five-year deal in excess of $40 million. From their point of view, he was a thirty-five-year-old pitcher with a history of back trouble.

So Cashman was in a situation much like a fighter comfortably ahead on points late in the bout who only has to make sure to play defense. He may have been in his first GM job and he may have been only thirty-one, but Cashman didn't waste his ten years in the Yankees world checking America Online and redoing his résumé.

Cashman's list of contacts was large. And it came in very handy when he was put in charge of making sure the Indians didn't get their hands on Johnson. The Boss could live with Johnson going to Anaheim or the Dodgers, teams he was rumored to be headed for. But not the Indians.

It was delicious irony that the Yanks would be in Seattle on Friday night, July 31. Adding a touch that even the most smarmy Hollywood script writer couldn't have cooked up, Hideki Irabu was slated to face the Mariners in a game as the deadline approached.

Despite the Yankees efforts to keep their talks secret, the word leaked out. If the Mariners GM Woody Woodward was going to deal Johnson to the defensive-minded Yankees, Irabu was the main ingredient.

Irabu made sense on a lot of fronts for the Mariners. One, of the $12.8 million Steinbrenner bestowed on him, Irabu had collected $8 million. Two, he had turned his career around, after a miserable 1997 season, to become an above-average major league starter who was certainly better than his No. 5 role with the Yankees. Three, the Mariners had Asian ownership and figured Irabu would be a drawing card in Seattle, which has a sizable Asian population.

Of course, there were other names in the mix. The Mariners also wanted pitcher Ramiro Mendoza, pitching prospect Ryan Bradley, and they loved third base prospect Mike Lowell and outfield prospect Ricky Ledee. Later they would ask for minor league first baseman Nick Johnson.

If all the Yankees were doing was keeping Johnson

away from the Indians, the price was certainly going to be steep.

As for the deadline, it was twelve P.M., New York time. That meant it was going to nine o'clock in Seattle. With the game starting at 7:05 local time, Irabu could be pitching the fifth inning.

Then, as if Cashman needed another card in the mix, a simple sentence uttered by Joe Torre after a 9–3 victory over the Angels on July 28 added it.

"He had trouble getting loose," Torre said, referring to David Cone.

What happened was, the Yankees took advantage of three Angel errors in the sixth to score three unearned runs. Cone, pitching that night, went to Torre and pitching coach Mel Stottlemyre after that long inning and told them that his arm was a little stiff, from the lengthy time he'd spent on the bench in a shirt drenched with sweat.

Nevertheless, Cone worked the seventh, and hiked his record to 15–3, before turning it over to Mike Stanton for the final two innings. Backed by home runs from Derek Jeter, Darryl Strawberry, and Bernie Williams, Cone had used his split-fingered fastball to keep the Angels, a team that feasts on fastballs, off balance.

"Best splitter I have had in a while," he said afterward, unaware that Torre had told the media about the getting loose problem. "I still felt good and I could have gone out there, but this year I'm trying to be more cautious. I don't want to happen what happened last year."

In 1997, Cone's season had ended with his right shoulder barking from August tendinitis.

The immediate outcome of this, and of Torre's simple utterance—"He had trouble getting loose"—was that suddenly it appeared the Yankees might have a reason to make a deal for Randy Johnson other than to keep him away from the Indians.

So with Johnson trade rumors engulfing their universe, the Yankee players continued to block things out. The thinking was: If Johnson arrives in a few days, fine. If not, well, it's not like there's a crying need for another starter on the best pitching staff in baseball.

"It's amazing, we're so conditioned to handle whatever comes our way," Cone said. "We've suffered devastating losses in the playoffs and won a World Series. We're ready for anything, and we know anything could happen."

As for the Johnson Saga, which thankfully would expire by midnight New York time the following night, it could only be classified as Seattle Confusion.

One minute the Mariners were ready to trade the Big Unit, the next, an owner—believed to be either Chris Larsen or Howard Lincoln—wanted to hang onto the flamethrowing lefty. Immediately after they lost, the Mariners were inclined to deal. When they won, they wanted to hold onto him and make a run for first place in the A.L. West, something they were nine games out of.

In the July 28 edition of the *Seattle Post-Intelligencer*, there was a report that Steinbrenner was willing to offer Johnson, a free agent after the season, a three-year deal, and that the Boss had offered Hideki Irabu, Darren Holmes, and Mike Lowell to the Mariners in exchange.

"Nothing to that," Cashman said. "Nothing at all."

The next day the buzz out of Seattle was that the Mariners wanted Ramiro Mendoza subbed for Holmes and were willing to expand the deal to include right-handed reliever Mike Timlin. The Yankees had had their eye on Timlin since Jeff Nelson was shelved with a back injury in late June. They might have been willing to part with Homer Bush for Timlin.

Meanwhile, the circus was expected to be at a fever pitch the next night at the Kingdome for the first of a three-game series against the Mariners. Yankee advance scouts Wade Taylor and Bob Didier had been watching the Mariners for days, and no doubt keeping separate eyes on Johnson and Timlin.

The confusion in Seattle wasn't limited to the Johnson Saga. In the past forty-eight hours the Mariners had talked to the Marlins about acquiring Todd Zeile to plug a hole at third base. But they weren't crossing off Russ Davis, the incumbent at third. And since Lowell was considered the Yankees third baseman of the future, it made some people wonder just what GM Woody Woodward was thinking. Later, it came out that Woodward had a trade set with the Marlins in which Lowell would be dealt to his hometown team.

What you didn't have to wonder about was how the Yankees wanted it to play out. In a perfect Yankee world, the Mariners would have rejected the Indians bid and a late push by the Red Sox and kept Johnson. That way Cashman wouldn't hear from Woodward late the following night, wanting to know if the Boss would top a Tribe or Bosox package.

As for Cone, well, he was listening to his head—stubborn at many times throughout a sterling career—instead of his huge heart. A year ago, he would have pitched through and not told Torre anything. This year, he didn't want the music to end in August. This time, Cone had plans on pitching deep into October.

With or without Johnson.

Meanwhile, on July 29, the Angels crushed Orlando "El Duque" Hernandez 10–5. El Duque, who fell to 5–3, gave up ten runs and thirteen hits in 3 1/3 innings as the Angels laid off his breaking stuff and feasted on an average fastball.

Combined with Torre saying Cone had "trouble getting loose," El Duque's subpar outing gave the impression Johnson could be needed after all.

Before pulling out of Anaheim, Andy Pettitte supplied seven shutout innings and outpitched Yankee-killer Chuck Finley 3–0. Pettitte allowed seven hits.

Now, the best team in baseball, still with a fifteen game lead over the Red Sox, made their way up the Pacific Coast to the Kingdome to face a Mariner team that had given up on the season.

As Friday dawned very clear, the Big Unit saga became more muddled by the hour.

Unless the Yankees were willing to part with another starting pitcher instead of Hideki Irabu in order to land Randy Johnson, the Mariners weren't going to send the Big Unit to the Bombers by the deadline.

While acquiring Irabu as part of a package that also included Mike Lowell for Johnson was intriguing on several fronts to the Mariners, manager Lou Piniella was against getting Irabu after the Mariners manager conducted a background check.

According to sources, Piniella was turned off by Irabu's temper, which he has controlled much better this season, as well as by reports that Irabu paid little attention to physical conditioning. Piniella was also informed that despite Irabu's efforts to portray himself in a better light this year, he often reverted to the surly hurler he was last year.

"Lou did some checking and found out a few things he didn't think would work out," the source said.

So, with the Yankees refusing to part with Andy Pettitte, and the Mariners not convinced that Ramiro Mendoza was a full-time starter, it was believed the Bombers were going to finish second to the package the Indians were prepared to present to Mariner GM Woody Woodward.

And that was Cashman's biggest nightmare as the hours crept toward the midnight deadline. Remember, George Steinbrenner's No. 1 interest in acquiring the strikeout king with a 9–10 record and 4.35 ERA was keeping Johnson away from the Indians, who had become the Boss's obsession.

Even with Irabu in the Yankees package, it may not have been enough to top the Indians offer. They were going to sacrifice left fielder Brian Giles, pitcher Chad Ogea, second baseman Enrique Wilson, and one of two minor league pitching studs, Willie Martinez or Tim Drew.

The Indians were so confident that they had a deal with the Mariners that they had minor leaguer Steve Karsay at the team hotel in Oakland ready to take Ogea's big league roster spot.

Meanwhile, the wild card in the picture were the Dodgers. On Thursday, the Indians believed the Dodgers were prepared to offer the Mariners a package that would smother theirs. However, concerning the Dodgers, there was subsequently minimal noise through the grapevine after the initial rumors. However, that would change.

Late Thursday night the Dodgers were ready to acquire Carlos Perez and Mark Grudzielanek from the

Expos. When the Mariners found out what GM Tommy Lasorda was offering—supposedly reliever Antonio Osuna, second baseman Wilton Guerrero, and minor league pitcher Ted Lilly—they told the Dodgers to hold the phone because they liked that package.

"The Dodgers went into a panic yesterday because the Giants acquired Ellis Burks and Joe Carter within a week," a source said of San Francisco, which was ahead of the Dodgers in the N.L. wild card chase.

So, with the Yankees prepared to face the Mariners at the Kingdome, and with Irabu starting, no less, they waited around not knowing if Johnson was hours away from joining them on a voyage that Steinbrenner demanded had to lead at least to the World Series.

While most Yankees just shrugged when asked about the prospects of Johnson upgrading the best staff in the American League and quite possibly all of baseball, Andy Pettitte wasn't doing cartwheels over the idea.

"I am definitely curious about it," he said. "I don't want to be too negative about it but we got a great thing going here, and you're talking about trading three or four players. But in New York, you go with the flow. We still have to worry about playing baseball."

10

August Heat

Even though it was Hideki Irabu's second season in the big leagues, there were situations that were foreign to him. He understood America a lot more than he had a year ago, and he was adapting to it as well as could be expected.

However, when he turned on the television in his Seattle hotel room on July 30, Irabu admitted he was a bit confused. Since he was going to start Friday night, Irabu had been sent ahead of the team from Anaheim. It's an old baseball custom, based on the rationale that the starting pitcher would get additional rest, that not too many teams use anymore. But too often the team would arrive at the hotel and the pitcher's key still hadn't been picked up from the front desk. So nowadays most teams keep the next night's pitcher with them to prevent them from going AWOL or taking a minivacation.

Around the Yankees the joke was that Irabu and interpreter George Rose had been sent to Seattle to facilitate Irabu's search for housing. But as Irabu sat at his locker preparing for that night's start, he wasn't amused.

Irabu admitted he was aware that he was a major

Scott Brosius drives in the first—and winning—run of the Division Series. His clutch hitting and sparkling defense were crucial to the Yankees success. (*Photo by Spencer A. Burnett*/New York Post)

Shane Spencer continues his torrid home-run hitting with a moon shot in Game 2 against Texas. (*Photo by Nury Hernandez*/New York Post)

David Wells, who would go on to win the ALCS MVP, sprays champagne in the Yankee clubhouse after they swept Texas to win the series. (*Photo by Charles Wenzelberg*/New York Post)

David Cone watches as Darryl Strawberry's wife, Charisse, and her children throw the first pitch of the ALCS. Strawberry, suffering from colon cancer, was always on the minds of his teammates. (*Photo by Nury Hernandez*/New York Post)

Chuck Knoblauch's worst moment in the ALCS. While he argued a controversial call, Cleveland scored a run and went on to win Game 2, 4–1. (*Photo by Francis Specker*/New York Post)

The dejected Yankee bench at the end of Game 2, shortly after Knoblauch's mental blunder. (*Photo by Francis Specker*/New York Post)

Chili Davis's bat came alive with three RBIs in Game 5, helping the Yankees gain a 3–2 edge in the ALCS. (*Photo by Charles Wenzelberg*/New York Post)

Jeter, Knoblauch, Brosius, and Martinez begin celebrating their 9–5 victory over the Indians—and the Yankees 35th American League Pennant. (*Photo by Don Halasy*/New York Post)

Tino Martinez follows through on his grand slam in Game 1 of the World Series. It gave the Yanks a decisive 9–6 win and broke him out of his post-season slump. (*Photo by Bob Olen*/New York Post)

Scott Brosius hits his second home run of the night in Game 3 of the World Series, bringing the Yankees to a 5–3 victory. Brosius went on to become the World Series MVP. (*Photo by Charles Wenzelberg*/New York Post)

The 1998 World Champion Yankees celebrate after a four-game sweep, delivering a second World Championship to the Bronx in three years, and the 24th World Series title for the NY Yankees—the most championships won by a single franchise in any sport. (*Photo by Francis Specker*/New York Post)

part of the Yankees effort to land Randy Johnson. How could he not? Every time he turned on a television he saw his name connected with a trade to the Mariners. When he arrived at the Kingdome, that's all he heard his teammates talk about.

So, against that backdrop, Irabu took the mound against the Mariners wondering if he was in the final innings of a Yankee career that would have been very short.

"I saw that my name was mentioned a lot," Irabu said. "I know it was a complex situation, but in any situation I try to do my best."

Irabu wasn't sensational, but thanks to a fastball with juice and the ability to get ahead of the muscular Mariner hitters, he was able to walk away with a 5–3 victory. The win was the Yankees third in four games, hiking the best record in baseball to 76–27.

According to catcher Jorge Posada, who contributed two homers, Irabu was on a mission to prove to the Yankee brass that he belonged in pinstripes and not in the Pacific Northwest.

"I wanted to go out there and throw hard," said Irabu, who improved to 10–4 with a seven-inning effort in which he allowed three runs and six hits, three of which were solo homers. "This is a strong team and I wanted to be part of this team."

On August 1, Irabu could stop worrying. The Mariners sent Johnson to Houston for two minor leaguers and a minor leaguer to be named, widely believed to be a coup by Houston.

"I am glad it's over, one way or the other," Joe Torre said of the anticipation of the past few days. "It's ancient history and we can go about our business."

That business consisted of staying healthy. The Red Sox, still fifteen games behind in the A.L. East, weren't going to catch the Yankees at this point, who were moving smoothly toward clinching the division title. August would be a month for the Bombers to get their house in order for October as Bernie Williams chased his first batting title and David Cone and David Wells went after the Cy Young award.

The Yankees world returned to as normal as it can get. The day after the deal didn't go down, Wells fired a complete game eight-hitter to beat the Mariners 5–2 and improve his record to 13-2. Still, the hot topic was the Deal that Wasn't Made. And what people were talking about was how Cashman made his bones in the GM fraternity.

When George Steinbrenner introduced Cashman to the baseball universe as Bob Watson's replacement on February 3, the Boss predicted that the neophyte Cashman would mature into one of the best GMs he'd ever hired. Cashman, thirty years old then, was young. From experience, he only knew how things were done in the Bronx, but he was a shrewd and tough negotiator. In the final hours of the trading deadline, when the GM didn't bite on an Indians bluff and then didn't cave into the Mariners demands for Ramiro Mendoza in order to acquire Randy Johnson, Cashman made the Boss look clairvoyant.

"He was under a lot of heat to make the deal, if only to keep Johnson away from the Indians," a source said. "With Johnson going to Houston, Cashman looks real good. Real good."

And so did the Yankees. The best starting rotation in baseball remained intact, since the Mariners didn't believe

No. 4 starter Hideki Irabu and minor leaguers Ricky Ledee and Mike Lowell were enough for the Big Unit. In addition to the Yankee rotation not being upset, Cashman held onto Mendoza, a big favorite of Joe Torre, because he had outstanding stuff and the ability to start or relieve.

Keeping Johnson away from the Indians, Public Enemy No. 1 in the Boss's eyes, wasn't his only goal, Cashman admitted later. The Yankees were seduced by Johnson's blazing fastball, and considered adding it to their pitching mix even after it was apparent that the Tribe had folded late Friday afternoon.

"We wanted him to pitch for us," Cashman said, "but the price was just too high."

Like a proud parent, the Boss was beaming over the way Cashman orchestrated things.

"It was the best possible scenario for us," said minor league head Mark Newman, who spent the day monitoring the Johnson Saga with the Boss in Tampa. "He was very happy with it."

Why Mariners GM Woody Woodward wasn't satisfied by a package of Irabu, Lowell, and Ledee is a question every wired-on-caffeine Mariner fan in the Pacific Northwest asked themselves. Sure, when Johnson said he was looking for a multiyear contract, it scared away a lot of teams. But many believed Woodward, who'd been the Yankee GM when Cashman was still a Yankee intern, was on his way out after not getting more for the best left-handed pitcher in baseball. And if Irabu, whom Mariners manager Lou Piniella had his doubts about, wasn't a deal-sealer, what about the Indians package of Brian Giles, Chad Ogea, Enrique Wilson, and either Tim Drew or Willie Martinez? Certainly that, or a fraction of that, was better than what Woodward got.

As for Cashman, he was sorry about not being able to find right-handed bullpen help for Torre, who'd been without Jeff Nelson for five weeks and lost Darren Holmes to the DL. Cashman was hot on the Mariners Mike Timlin and was very interested in the Dodgers Antonio Osuna.

"I was disappointed," Cashman said of his failure to locate bullpen help. "But we hope Jeff Nelson can come back."

Nelson, the Yankees' right-handed setup man, had been on the DL since late June with a bulging disc in his lower back. He vowed to return by September 1, but hadn't done anything baseball-related since July 12. Holmes, too, had recently bowed out with the same ailment.

As for the twenty-six-year-old Mendoza, he was quickly turning into a name that either killed deals or stalled them. Last summer, the Royals wanted him for Chili Davis and were rebuffed. This past February, the Twins insisted he be included in the Chuck Knoblauch deal before finally realizing the Yankees weren't going to do it. Friday night, after talking to Torre, Cashman refused to part with Mendoza.

When told he was the reason Randy Johnson wasn't a Yankee, the soft-spoken right-hander said, "Good, I am glad."

And what about not having to see Johnson in an Indians uniform? Did that brighten Joe Torre's night?

"You bet," he said. "If we have to face Randy now, it's in the World Series, and I'll take my chances."

The final leg of the Yankees West Coast trip was Oakland, where they would play four games in three days. In the first game, they rode a seventeen-hit attack, highlighted by two Knoblauch homers and one each by Paul O'Neill and Darryl Strawberry, to a 14–1 victory. The offensive orgy made El Duque Hernandez's night very comfortable. He improved to 6–3 with a complete game three-hitter.

The river of hits continued to flow the next night when Knoblauch and Strawberry again went deep in the first game of a doubleheader won by the Yankees, 10–3. When they took the field for the nightcap at Oakland Coliseum, the Yankees didn't know that their manager had used them and the legendary 1976 Cincinnati Reds in the same sentence.

Their relentless approach to every at-bat was proof that they thought no further than the next pitch they saw. Having been asked since early June to explain their phenomenal success, the players politely stated their only goal as reaching the World Series. Nothing else mattered, they said. The all-time win mark was for others to talk about, since they were perfectly content to dig in against the slop being slung their way. So it was somewhat surprising to hear Joe Torre compare his Bombers to the Big Red Machine that had terrorized National League pitchers in the mid-seventies.

"The 1976 Reds," Torre said when asked between games if he could recall a club as dominant as his. "And I think we have better pitching than them."

The Big Red Machine is considered one of the great all-time teams. While Torre's lineup didn't have a Hall of Famer in it, Anderson's had two in Joe Morgan and Johnny Bench. Anderson also had Pete Rose, who should be in Cooperstown, and Tony Perez, a borderline candidate.

But when it came to pitching, Torre was right: his are

better. Don Gullett was Anderson's ace. On this Yankee staff he would be no better than a fourth starter. Where do you think Pat Zachry, Gary Nolan, and Jack Billingham would fit into Torre's rotation? Move to the bullpen and it's an even bigger mismatch. Rawley Eastwick was Anderson's closer and had 26 saves. On the Yankees, Mariano Rivera was on a pace to post forty. Other bullpen names Anderson dialed often were Freddy Norman, Pedro Borbon, and Will McEnaney. But Anderson didn't have the luxury of a Ramiro Mendoza to insert into the rotation, as Torre did for the first game of the Oakland twinbill, the night comparisons between his team and the Big Red Machine was broached.

But those Reds won the World Series in 1975 and 1976, so until the Yankees win their second title in three years, such talk was a bit premature. But was there anything else to rap about when it came to the Yankees?

"Pitching is definitely the reason," Torre reiterated, concerning his comparison. "Because [the Reds] found so many ways to beat you, with power and batting average. In a lot of ways, it's similar to what we do."

Torre had no way of knowing that power would carry his club to a scintillating victory in the second game at Oakland that night, with the Yankees scoring nine runs in the ninth.

Old friend Kenny Rogers had taken a 5–1 lead into the ninth before Tino Martinez and Tim Raines singled. In came A's closer Billy Taylor to face Chad Curtis. The move appeared to be the right one when Taylor induced Curtis to hit a perfect double play ball right at Mike Blowers. However, the ball went under Blowers's glove and between his legs. Instead of having two outs and a runner on third, Taylor was looking at loaded bases, no outs, and Strawberry hitting for Joe Girardi.

Taylor started Strawberry off with a first-pitch breaking ball for a strike and then ran the count to 2–2. Strawberry fouled off another breaking ball, and Taylor, not wanting to hang another, threw a fastball that Strawberry lined over the center-field fence for his second pinch-hit grand slam of the season. His other one had come in Kansas City on May 2. Strawberry is the only Yankee ever to hit two slams off the bench in the same season. That's an A.L. record and ties the major league mark.

"Joe told me that if Curtis got on, I was going to be the hitter," Strawberry said. "Give Joe Torre the credit, he put me in the situation. I knew I hit it good, but you never know about line drives, sometimes they aren't homers."

With twenty homers and a .266 batting average, Strawberry had not only helped the Yankees to their big lead in the A.L. East, he had reestablished himself as a force at the plate. But Chili Davis's return was on the horizon, as everyone knew. In fact, he came back less than two weeks later. While Strawberry's bat was screaming, his lips were sealed. He'd let his lumber do the talking, and if that wasn't good enough to continue to play when Davis came back, well, that was the way it was going to be. There would be no ranting and raving from Strawberry.

"Nothing you can do about it," he said. "Joe is the manager and I do what he wants. You just have to look at it that when Chili comes back, he'll help us win games too."

There was a time when a sideways glance from a

manager would set Strawberry off. Now, older, more mature, and sober, he understood everything a lot clearer. He might not have liked taking a seat, but who would, after what Strawberry had accomplished this season after missing almost all of 1997 due to knee surgery.

"It's just what we've been preparing for," Torre said of Davis's return. "Darryl may feel well enough to play the outfield. But we're going to have to get Chili at-bats. If not, there's no sense activating him. The players will understand that now is the time to see what kind of ammunition we have."

Yankee Profile:
Chuck Knoblauch

Eyes don't have to be moist to show pain. Tears don't have to trickle down a cheek to portray the hurt that pulls at the heart.

To see Chuck Knoblauch at his Legends Field locker in the early days of spring training, you would think his world was perfect. He was a Yankee with a beautiful wife, millions of dollars and more green on the horizon. Who could ask for more?

How about having a conversation with Ray Knoblauch? Have Dad fully understand his youngest son wears the most famous uniform in baseball. Have the man who threw batting practice and hit fungoes to you from the time you could walk understand the new chapter in your baseball life. Get more than a one-word answer from your Bellaire High School baseball coach who held the job for twenty-five years.

The money and recognition are what the public sees. But they can't do a thing about a father suffering from Alzheimer's disease.

"It's been really hard," Knoblauch told the *Post*. "You can't pick up the phone and talk to Dad normally. You have to ask yes or no questions. It's tough and definitely on my mind. Obviously, he has been a big part of my life and big part of my baseball career."

Ray Knoblauch, former minor leaguer pitcher, has been battling the insidious disease for six years. Able to ride a bike and participate in a game of catch as he did two weeks ago in Houston, Ray Knoblauch, seventy, is limited to short answers.

"I had him at the batting cage and I turned to ask him if everything looked okay and all he could do was say, 'Yes,'" said a choked-up Chuck Knoblauch.

And what about the son being a Yankee?

"I think he knows, but there is no way for me to know that he knows because of the communication problem," Chuck said.

"It's been very difficult because it's such a complicated and strange disease. It's hard to figure out," Chuck added. "You just hope to maintain a certain phase as long as you can."

As is often the case when one parent is ill, the offspring worries about the spouse.

"My mom [Linda] is the primary care giver for him, so we are somewhat concerned about her health," the son said. "If she doesn't stay healthy, then both of them . . . "

The voice trails toward Scott Brosius's locker to the right. The eyes remain dry but there is a catch in the voice. The Adam's apple is bigger.

"It's mind-boggling and a very strange disease," he continued. "I have come to know it pretty well."

Well enough to understand that it could run in the family of four kids Ray and Linda raised. When Chuck had Ray examined at the Mayo Clinic in 1996, the doctors removed a sample from Ray's brain.

"We agreed to let them do that, and at the autopsy they can find out if that's what it is [hereditary]," Chuck said. "There's a test [for younger people], but they shy away from doing it because if you were thirty years old, would you want to know?"

So the phone in the Houston home rings every day, the son wanting to know how the father is doing. Early in 1998 the conversations centered around bringing Ray Knoblauch to see Chuck's first spring training as a Yankee.

"At this time of year, I will start talking about spring training and he will get excited," Chuck said. "I think we're going to try and get him down here for a couple of weeks. He asks my mom every day if spring training started yet. He doesn't say the whole word, but . . . "

For Chuck Knoblauch there's more than enough to remind him the man Ray was. He looks around at the names above the lockers at Legends Field and knows Ray played a part in him being here.

"There is a tape, a reel-to-reel thing from 1972 when I was at one of his games, and the bats are bigger than me and I'm dragging them around," Chuck Knoblauch said. "As far back as I can recall, I remember being around baseball and being around him. God gives everybody some talent but there's a lot to say about being around the game and getting the right direction."

Today the son—rich beyond his wildest imaginings and living the dream of every little boy—watches his father move slowly in the wrong direction without the power to do a thing about it, other than to hope.

There's nothing that speaks more loudly or dangerously through the baseball brotherhood than a whisper. If you were plugged into the dingy corners of the chamber this past February, after Chuck Knoblauch was acquired by the Yankees for a quartet of prospects, the message being put out on the double-knit information highway was this: Knoblauch was a talented but selfish player. Of course, no names were attached to the whispers filtering from Minneapolis to New York.

Other people around the Twins chuckled when they heard that the ultra-intense Knoblauch was headed for the media capital of the world.

No matter how hard they strive to live in a bubble, the inhabitants of the Yankees clubhouse hear the murmurs because there is no bigger gossip network on the planet than big league players. Even the ones who don't kick in, hear the dirt. They waited to see if the boisterous noises being delivered by phantom voices were carrying the truth. Sure, Knoblauch was a stud player, a .304 career hitter, a Gold Glove winner, a four-time All-Star and member of the 1991 World Champion Twins. But they wanted to see how he fit into a room swollen with players who check egos and attitudes at the door 162 times a year and do whatever it takes to win that night.

Four months into a season that had a chance to be the best ever in baseball history, the Yankees were wondering if the words in those whispers were describing Knoblauch.

"In this game, you hear people say things about people all the time," said Darryl Strawberry, who has had plenty of whispering done in front of and behind his back. "But Chuck is a gamer, a guy who loves the game. He has a great attitude about him because he hates—and I mean hates—to lose. He hates when he doesn't do well. I know he isn't content with the year he's having and that's good. He could have come here and accepted things, but he doesn't."

The first half of Knoblauch's initial season in pinstripes was a rocky one. The .304 lifetime hitter was hitting .263 at the All-Star break. To accept that kind of dropoff would be going against everything Knoblauch is about. Being a member of the best team in baseball certainly didn't mean he'd embrace 0–for–5 nights.

Twice during the year Knoblauch's emotions led him to admit he "hadn't contributed anything" to the Yankees success and that he was "tired of stinking out the joint."

But he made no excuses for the batting average or a problem throwing to first base that plagued him early in the season. Nor did he once lean on his father's illness as a crutch. Knoblauch also ignored the talk that he put too much pressure on himself to do well in his first year as a Yankee, much the way Tino Martinez did when he followed Don Mattingly into the Bronx in 1996. And he never mentioned that he had the contractual right to escape the Yankees via a trade or free agency before next season starts.

"At times I think I'm ready to break out, and then it doesn't happen," said the second baseman, who watched hours of tape from when he hit .341 in 1996. "It comes and goes and I don't know why."

If Knoblauch beat himself up over his performance on the field, he didn't let it show to his teammates.

"As a player, you look for things like how the stars react when they don't get a hit the whole game," said Dale Sveum, who has spent a lot of time on major league benches observing everything. "There are some guys who pout. Chuck never pouts. He is always into the game no matter what kind of game he is having. That's how you judge people."

Of course, winning cures everything. But is it that simple? Was Knoblauch a victim of a smear campaign orchestrated by Minnesota Twins manager Tom Kelly's moles? Or did he make an effort to get along with the galaxy of stars in the Yankees world after spending too many years of drowning in the sea of mediocrity the Twins always sail on?

"Winning is everything," Knoblauch said. "And everybody here has made it very easy to feel comfortable."

In return, Knoblauch has done things to make you wonder about the whispers that he was a hostile island in the middle of the Twins clubhouse.

Early in the season, when the Yankees plane from Seattle landed at Newark Airport at five A.M., Knoblauch hadn't seen the Manhattan apartment his wife Lisa had moved them into. He knew senior adviser Arthur Richman, who does not drive, lives in Greenwich Village, and he offered Richman a ride from his car service. It's a practice Knoblauch continued throughout the year.

"I said to him, 'I thought you were supposed to be a red-ass,'" Richman said. "This guy is as genuine as they get. You judge people on how they treat you, and he has treated me great, and who am I?"

Once, from across the Yankee clubhouse, Scott Brosius came to Knoblauch's locker carrying a cell phone in a box. Knoblauch had hooked the All-Star third baseman up with a deal, and Brosius wanted to know the specifics.

To Joe Torre, Knoblauch was the pest who hit .400 (18-for-45) against the Yankees last year. So when the Yankees shipped Eric Milton, Brian Buchanan, Cristian Guzman, and Danny Mota to the Twins for Knoblauch, Torre was elated.

Asked in late January about the whispers, Torre said he would wait and see for himself. After the season started he was asked again. What about it, Joe?

"Selfish?" Torre asked. "What's selfish? He gets mad after he makes an out, but that's not bad, that's not selfish. He doesn't show his emotions the way Paulie [O'Neill] does, but he gets upset. But he isn't selfish. He's done everything we've asked from him as a leadoff man. He's set the tone and has made pitchers pitch to [Derek] Jeter."

A thin smile creased Chad Curtis's face when he was asked about the whispers.

"I heard the same thing about me when I got here," said Curtis, who refers to Knoblauch as Chuckles and shares Knoblauch's strong interest in diet and vitamin intake. "He gets mad because he makes an out, but what he's mad about is that he's let the team down. I've seen guys mad because their average dips, and Chuck isn't like that."

Paul O'Neill said: "When they talked about getting him, I thought he would be the perfect piece of the puzzle they were putting together. I still think that way."

Finally, there's David Cone's take on Knoblauch. Cone has seen just about every type of player walk through a big league clubhouse. So what about the whispers, David?

"The guy is a gamer," Cone said. "Selfish? I haven't seen one iota of that."

Gamer. In a galaxy where whispers scream, there's no greater compliment. It's no secret that Knoblauch wasn't the complete player the Yankees thought they were getting. Perhaps more importantly, he hasn't been the person the whispers said he was.

The image Scott Nethery has of Chuck Knoblauch isn't the one we see. Having known Knoblauch since he was a kid, Nethery has a different perspective on what makes Knoblauch tick. Where we see the opposite-field stroke, the stolen bases, and the Gold Glove defense, Nethery remembers the will to win that raged inside Knoblauch.

Nethery is a scout for the Atlanta Braves who played at Houston's Bellaire for Chuck's legendary father, Ray, and coached Chuck as a teenager. "He knew how to play the game when he was a little, biddy kid," Nethery said. "He used to get mad at the other kids because he always knew what was happening on the field and where to go, and they didn't."

Where does that type of fire start? Why does it burn so brightly in the belly of one child and not the next? How does it continue to boil as the boy moves from kid to teenager to adult to multimillionaire big leaguer? And when does it end?

In Knoblauch's case, he believes it's a combination of his mother and father.

"Out of the womb, I guess," he said when asked where he acquired the competitive attitude that eventually led to him asking out of the downtrodden world of the Twins. "Hanging around my dad's teams, he was always a winning coach. I grew up expecting to see his teams win all the time. There was also a passion for playing baseball and wanting to get better and better at it. That has to go hand in hand with it. If you're doing something you like, you want to succeed."

Throughout his baseball life, Knoblauch has tasted success. He won at Bellaire, played an integral part on a 1984 Mickey Mantle national championship team, and won again at Texas A&M.

So when the Twins won the World Series in 1991, the season in which Knoblauch was A.L. Rookie of the Year, he was blind-sided by what followed a 92–70 record in 1992.

"That was my toughest year ever," Knoblauch said of the 1993 season, when the Twins finished 71–91 and 23 games out. "It was so hard and I didn't understand it. We won the World Series in 1991, and in 1992 we just missed the play-offs. It was tough to stay focused and concentrate on what had to be done. I learned so much from that year. I wasted at-bats and lost concentration on defense."

The biggest lesson remained with Knoblauch through 1994, 1995, 1996, and 1997. By the middle of the 1997 season, despite being in the first year of a five-year, $30 million deal, Knoblauch decided to waive his no-trade clause.

Yes, he wanted out of a losing situation. No, he didn't tell the Twins to deal him or else.

"What people have missed," Knoblauch pointed out, "is that I didn't demand a trade, I asked for one."

There was a time in Knoblauch's career when every out resulted in a helmet being tossed or a bat broken.

"I used to be one of those snap guys, I think everybody has it in them," Knoblauch admitted. "I try to learn something every year, and throughout the years you realize there's going to be another day and you realize you're going to get who knows how many more plate appearances. I would like to think I've calmed down from my first year."

However, not to the point where he'll accept losing. With the Yankees, that wasn't a concern.

11

Dominating to the End .

Avoid injury. See what Chili Davis could provide. Find out if Jeff Nelson's bothersome back was going to hold up. And clinch the A.L. East. If setting a win record or two was a by-product of that plan, well, it would be nice. But Joe Torre made it very clear that he wasn't going to jeopardize a successful October chasing the 1927 Yankees, the 1954 Indians, and the 1906 Cubs.

Babe Ruth's 1927 Yankees, considered by many the benchmark that every other team has been measured against, bagged a Yankee record of 110 wins. The 1954 Indians, the team George Steinbrenner has committed to memory since he watched it as a boy in Cleveland, won 111 games to set the A.L. record. The 1906 Cubs reached 116 wins, which was the most ever.

Of the three record-holders, only the 1927 Yankees won a World Series. It wasn't something Torre harped on, but he knew the drill around the Yankees: win the World Series or the year isn't considered a success. Sit on top of the hill and nobody cared how many regular season games you won.

So, nobody appreciated Steinbrenner saying records didn't matter more than Torre. As long as the Boss is on board, things always tend to go smoother. However, on August 12 the Yankees were an intoxicating 86–29 and their lead over the Red Sox had swelled to 17 1/2 games. And while the Boss isn't from Missouri, he often says he has to be shown results before he believes. Now, he'd seen the results, and the architect of the best team in baseball was pleased.

Of course, there had been the danger of the Boss getting caught up in the record hunt. Steinbrenner is a man who loves to win. He never apologizes for his thirst for victory or the means he employs to sip from the chalice of winners. It was instilled at a very young age by his father that winning was very important. Second place was for the other guy. That's what made his quotes on August 12 somewhat surprising, since the Boss is never a man to smell the coffee until it's completely brewed.

When May turned to June and all signs indicated the Yankees were preparing to deliver a baseball summer to remember, Steinbrenner warned that his club had accomplished absolutely nothing beyond turning around a 1–4 start. June melted into July and the message being sent from Tampa focused on October: the ring is the thing. July folded into August with the Yankees expected to make a serious run at the record books, and the song remained the same. And while the Boss says winning the World Series has been his goal from Day 1 and remains in his cross hairs, he had come to appreciate the dominance of his club.

"I wouldn't be disappointed, they shouldn't be disappointed, and the city shouldn't be disappointed if they don't go all the way," the Boss told the *Post*. "We will certainly try our best to do that, but there is nothing to be ashamed of this year."

As a Scott Brosius seventh-inning home run climbed toward Monument Park and helped the Yankees to an 11–2 victory over the Twins, the monster of Yankee Stadium roared with approval. Now, as Brosius rounded the bases after stepping all over the Twins throats with both sets of cleats, Steinbrenner had a question.

"What just happened?" Steinbrenner asked the *Post*.

Informed that Brosius had homered, the Boss replied, "Unbelievable."

Steinbrenner was reacting to the latest beating administered by his club, but he could have easily been talking about the entire season.

"I can't explain it," Steinbrenner said of his 87–29 club, which had won seven straight, ten of eleven, and nineteen of 23 after punishing the hapless Twins. "In my twenty-five years in the game and forty years in athletics, I have never seen anything like this. I don't want it to come to an end."

It didn't figure to anytime soon because not one Yankee regular besides Brosius was having a career year, which pleased the Boss.

"It's getting done by a different guy every game," Steinbrenner said. "It really has nothing to do with chemistry, because as I have said all along, team chemistry is built by winning."

Unsolicited, the Boss said he saw a little bit of the midseventies Reds in his club because of the way they annihilated teams. During the seven-game winning streak, the Yankees outscored the Royals and Twins 66–14.

"If I can compare them to a team, it would be the Big Red Machine," the Boss said. "They rolled over everybody."

As proud as Steinbrenner was that his team was the

talk of baseball, he wanted the grunts of the organization to receive their due for helping to assemble the best
baseball team on the planet.

"I hope the people who worked hard are remembered," he said of his Inner Circle. "Mark Newman,
Gene Michael, Brian Cashman. Lin Garrett, Billy Connors, and Gordon Blakeley. These guys were there every
step of the way when we put this team together."

Now the Boss watched his team walk over the competition and realized that no matter how October turned out,
the summer delivered by Joe Torre's band of quiet assas-
sins had been something special. That, of course, could
change with an October disaster, but for now, one of the
hardest men in America to please understood all that
money he spent hadn't gone to waste. Nothing in Steinbrenner's appreciation speech hinted he was suddenly
looking to set records. Still, his appetite to be the best
might surface as the Yankees closed in on some milestones.

But when the Yankees lost three of the first five September games, talk of chasing down the 1906 Cubs
stalled. Privately, Torre was thankful. So too were a lot
of other people in the organization, because nobody
wanted a postseason opponent to have more motivation
to beat the Yankees. Taking out the Yankees was always
pleasing to other teams in the major league, but if they
were the best regular season team ever, it would make it
that much sweeter.

When they dropped three straight from September 5
through 7, the Yankees had lost eleven of nineteen and
just about killed all chatter about the 1906 Cubs. By
September 9 the Yankees magic number had been
reduced to one. That meant if they beat the Red Sox at
Fenway Park that night, they would clinch their second

A.L. East title in three years. To their loyal fans, the vision of Yankees celebrating in New England's living room while the Red Sox fans watched was delicious. The Orioles had replaced the Red Sox as the Yankees biggest A.L. East rival, and the Indians had forged their way past the Red Sox by beating the Yankees in the 1997 A.L. Division Series. Still, it was the Red Sox, and there wasn't a Yankee fan alive who hadn't heard or participated in a Yankee Stadium chant of "Boston sucks."

Since the middle of May the Yankees had been expected to win. And as the summer stretched out and their lead grew, it was only a matter of when they would clinch. When they locked up a playoff spot via the wild card on the last Saturday in August, the players didn't know it until the next day. That's how little it meant to them.

And with the emphasis on winning the World Series so prevalent throughout the organization, not much of a celebration was expected when Derek Jeter gobbled up John Valentin's grounder and fired to first baseman Tino Martinez for the final out of a 7–5 victory that clinched the pennant.

As the Yankees gathered on the mound, they shook hands and exchanged hugs. Nothing in their actions gave you the impression that in ten minutes their cramped clubhouse would be turned into a scene from *Animal House*.

Victory never smelled worse.

A trifecta of champagne, cigar smoke, and beer had turned the already musty air of the Fenway Park visitor's clubhouse into the main room of a fraternity house the morning after. With a 7–5 win in one pocket, their second divisional title in three years in the other, and hats commemorating the moment on their heads, the most stoic team in baseball let a season's worth of emotion spill out of their systems. For one hour they celebrated what they all hoped was the first step on their way to a World Championship.

So what if the baseball universe expected them to win the A.L. East from St. Patrick's Day on? Who cared if the *Post* declared the A.L. East over on May 25 when it printed that the magic number was 112. The Yankees had put together a remarkable summer, and now it was time to enjoy it.

"This is the reason I signed here," veteran switch-hitter Chili Davis said off to the side of the raucous celebration being held in the middle of a clubhouse smaller than some two-car Long Island garages. "I knew one way or another this would happen, that the Yankees would be playing after the end of the season."

Who they would play in the A.L. Division Series was still in question. But that was for later on. Now, it was Jeff Nelson, towering over everybody but Graeme Lloyd, letting champagne flow. Or Jorge Posada, catching instructor Gary Tuck, and minor league call-up Mike Figga, waiting an hour to soak the veteran Joe Girardi.

Everybody but George Steinbrenner, who slipped out a side door and onto the team bus, was soaked. Even bench coach Don Zimmer, who thought the shower stalls would be a nice place to stay dry, drowned in an ocean of Freixferet Brut, courtesy of Davis.

"This is a great feeling, we have to enjoy what we have accomplished so far," said Bernie Williams, who thought he was safe from the madness until Posada ambushed him. In a corner. "There are other things out there, but who knows what happens? The year we had, we have to stop for a minute and enjoy ourselves."

Yes, the year they were having. The victory allowed them to be the earliest Yankee team to clinch a title since the inception of divisional play in 1969. The 1941 Yankees clinched the American League pennant on September 4 for the earliest clinch date.

It also pushed their record to 102–41 and kept them within reach of the A.L. record of 111 wins set by the 1954 Indians, and the Yankee mark of 110 set by the 1927 Bombers.

Of course, when Steinbrenner and his Inner Circle began putting this team together after Williams's fly ball to Brian Giles resulted in a loss to the Indians in Game 5 of last year's A.L. Division Series, they weren't thinking only about copping the A.L. East. No, as always, the Boss wants it all. It's a message that is well-received in the clubhouse.

"Hopefully, it's the first step," said Derek Jeter, who, with Paul O'Neill, homered twice. "We still have a long way to go."

While the celebration was high-spirited, it was within reason.

"We wanted to be in control, but we didn't want to downplay it," David Cone said. "It's a cause for celebration, but we definitely wanted to show some class."

The last time there were this many Yankees in one room where alcohol was being served was immediately after they arrived home from Cleveland after the Game 5 loss. At a bar on Fourteenth Street in Manhattan, the Yankees gathered to wash away the awful taste of defeat.

"This is the first step," Cone said of erasing what the

Yankees felt that October night. "When you look back to that devastating loss and all the work it took to get to this point, it makes it all the more gratifying."

While O'Neill wasn't a big participant in the booze showers, he was proud of their achievement.

"When you win your division, it's a big accomplishment," O'Neill said. "We played hard all year to wrap this thing up early and be ready when October comes."

The remaining days couldn't drop off the calendar soon enough for the Yankees. Normally after a team clinches, the regulars get a few days off and the September call-ups get playing time. But since Torre was aware the Blue Jays and Red Sox were battling for the A.L. wild card slot in the playoffs, he basically played his "A" team against the Blue Jays in the following four games at Yankee Stadium, and lost three of them. Yes, he rested a few stars, but not all of them.

Orlando Hernandez got the ship righted by beating Pedro Martinez and the Red Sox 3–0, with a complete-game effort on September 14 at the Stadium. El Duque, a man who had experienced so much since leaving Cuba in late December on a small raft, was 10–4 and had proven to everybody that he had what it took to pitch in the big leagues.

The Red Sox bounced back the next night against Queens rookie Mike Jerzembeck, but nobody seemed to mind. However, when the lowly Devil Rays blanked the Bombers 7–0 on September 16 at Tropicana Field, the Yankees received a wake-up call from Torre the likes of which they'd never heard.

After three hours and eight minutes of watching the Yankees sleepwalk, Torre was displeased. He'd seen left fielder Chad Curtis throw to the wrong base in the fifth inning and take the wrong angle on a base hit in the eighth. He'd seen Graeme Lloyd walk Fred McGriff leading off the eighth, and rookie Shane Spencer not run hard to first in the sixth on a grounder to short. There was a spotty sixth inning from Andy Pettitte, and Bernie Williams swinging at a pitch over his head in the seventh.

Now, minutes after an embarrassing 7–0 loss to Tony Saunders, a 6–14 pitcher, Torre stood in the middle of a spacious clubhouse and let the A.L. East champions know he wasn't happy.

"Tonight was sloppy, it stunk," Torre said later of his club's fifth loss in six games. "I let them know about it. It stunk."

Torre isn't Billy Martin or Lou Piniella, former Yankee managers prone to losing their cool in front of players to the point where they embarrassed and enraged the players. Torre is a manager who rarely lets anyone see him sweat. And on the rare occasions he feels a need to raise his voice an octave or three, he usually waits until the next day.

However, watching the action, Torre had to let it go.

"You have to do it when you think you need to do it," Torre said about the short but effective meeting that followed after his team left eleven runners on base. "There are certain times when you want to talk about certain things. But when you get emotional, I guess it's better off for my health to get it out."

Moving through a very somber Yankee clubhouse, it was impossible to find a uniform who believed Torre was wrong in going to the whip two weeks before the postseason began.

"He told us, and everybody here knows it," said

Derek Jeter, who went 1–for–4 to extend a slump to 6–for–37 (.162), and implored the infield to get it going on the mound during a pitching change in the eighth inning. "We know how we're playing, and we know how we're capable of playing. It looks like we're going through the motions."

It was the fifth time during the season that the Bombers were blanked, and the loss dropped the best record in baseball to 104–46. The Devil Rays, who were 44 games behind the Yankees, upped their record to a dismal 60–90.

"We're all angry at ourselves," Joe Girardi said. "It's embarrassing the way we're playing. It's better to get our butts chewed out instead of not being sure about things. Hopefully, this is a wakeup call."

After Torre lit into them, the Yankees went 10–2 the rest of the way. They broke the 1927 Yankees record of 110 wins on September 24 with a 5–2 win over Tampa Bay. The next day they eclipsed the 1954 Indians A.L. record by winning their 112th game when they beat the Devil Rays 6–1.

They finished the season with a 114 victories and a seven-game winning streak. They also welcomed out-fielder Shane Spencer to the playoff roster after the rookie outfielder hit seven homers—three of them grand slams—in 28 at-bats. The collection of high-priced ballplayers with proven track records were amazed by Spencer, a 28th-round draft pick not many in the organization felt had a major league future. Spencer was yet another remarkable development in a season where fortune seemed to smile upon the Yankees.

• • •

The regular season had ended. October had arrived. All the hard work, all the strategizing, all the brilliance of a historic year wouldn't mean as much if the Yankees couldn't take it all. Within less than a month they could be World Champions. But there were obstacles, of course—other teams that, while maybe not as talented, were just as hungry. First up, the formidable, power-hitting Texas Rangers.

Yankee Profile:
Joe Torre and
Don Zimmer

Look at them together on the television screen and there are times when you wonder if they're two guys sitting at a bus stop dressed in similar suits who have never met each other. Yet, Joe Torre and Don Zimmer don't need to chat each other up every minute of the game. Zimmer knows he's the bench coach and Torre is the boss.

But there may not be a better relationship in baseball than what Torre and Zimmer have. Not close before Torre asked Zimmer to come aboard as his bench coach for the 1996 World Championship Series, the two have grown very, very close. They play golf together, go to the racetrack together, and together they run the best ship in baseball.

Unlike a lot of other managers, Torre relies on his coaches. It makes no difference what the pecking order. If catching coach Gary Tuck has an idea, Torre is open to it. Of course, Zimmer is different. He serves as Torre's sounding board as well as a person who offers opinions.

George Steinbrenner has had many managers, but none have enjoyed the relationship Torre has had with the Boss, who hired Torre on the recommendation of his senior adviser, Arthur Richman. Yes, he's been given horses with unbelievable breeding lines to ride, which makes it a little easier working for George Steinbrenner. But the barn was full of talent for Billy Martin, Bob Lemon, Dick Howser, and Lou Piniella, and things, shall we say, didn't go smoothly. So, what separates Torre from his predecessors?

Part of it may be due to Torre's unwillingness to get caught up in all the BS that surrounds the Yankees—which has decreased over the years, but is still there—and so he doesn't have to worry about things that don't affect him. Another part of it might be that Torre's secure in what he does; he doesn't worry about getting axed. When you've been sacked three times, what's one more pink slip?

Don Zimmer, with fifty years of baseball experience, has an informed opinion. Zimmer was a coach for Billy and Lou, and knows the effect an adversarial relationship between the manager's office and the Boss can have on a Yankee club.

"You ask me why he's the perfect man for this job, and the one main thing I can think of is that he gets along with Steinbrenner halfway decent," Zimmer explained on an early Chicago morning in the visitors' dugout at Comiskey Park. "It's not a hundred percent, but he has a way with George. I feel that has a lot to do with our club. The players fit with him and he's good for the players, that's what I see. He doesn't get too excited if George says something to him he doesn't like. He can come back with something because he knows how to handle George. They kind of get along, and that's a plus."

Torre was asked about his relationship with the Boss.

"I like to believe that we have a mutual respect for each other," he said. "I know he's the boss, but we can discuss things. You can't worry about every move you make. You have to do what you have to do."

Steinbrenner has said often that he feels as comfortable with Torre at the helm of his club than he has with any manager. That was evident this past July 31 when the Mariners insisted Ramiro Mendoza be included in a deal for Randy Johnson. Torre, who loves Mendoza's arm and versatility, lobbied hard for Mendoza not to be included, and he wasn't. Listening to wise old heads like Torre is something Steinbrenner has learned to do in recent years.

Fired by the Mets, Braves, and Cardinals, Torre arrived in the Bronx with a losing record and was immediately greeted by the nickname "Clueless Joe."

"What's the worst thing he can do, fire me?" Torre said when asked about working for Steinbrenner.

Since then Torre has piloted the Bombers into the playoffs the past three years, won two World Series, and has raised his managerial record over .500. Two World Series titles in three years have made Torre a prime candidate for Cooperstown via the Veterans Committee.

"This is the most fun I have had. Of course, 1996 was a lot of fun, but 1997 was a struggle right from spring training," Torre said of a club that was handicapped by the personal agendas of Charlie Hayes and Wade Boggs. "This has been great. We have stayed driven. Last year, after all we accomplished in '96, I was afraid I would be looked at as if I got mine and anything after this is gravy. I got tense and couldn't enjoy myself."

Even if the poker face remains stoic in the dugout, Torre has had a blast this summer. His lack of ego aside, he has quietly reveled in the fact that his club spent the entire year challenging the 1906 Cubs for the most wins ever. Being remembered as the best regular season Yankee team of all-time also had Torre smiling.

The poker face remained the same during the postseason, but we should have known that from the 1996 World Series, when he looked the Boss in the eye before the first two games against the Braves and told him the Yankees might lose the first two but they would sweep in Atlanta.

Right there it should have been clear that Torre was the Perfect Manager for the Imperfect Boss.

"I know it's an overused cliché, but the best thing about Joe is that he is so even-keeled," David Cone said. "He never panics, never. This is a veteran club, and he knows we know what it takes. Sure, there have been times when he reminds us of certain things, but he really is the right manager for this team."

According to GM Brian Cashman, a ten-year veteran of watching managers come and go in Yankee land, the way Torre deals with every aspect of his situation stands out.

"He handles New York in a quiet, relaxed way," Cashman said. "He is relaxed, but professional. He has an attitude that moves through the clubhouse. All the stuff that had been distractions in the past have gone away."

Torre isn't as soft as a pair of expensive leather shoes. He isn't homespun like Clyde King, and doesn't invite you to sit on a bench for hours and call you "Meat" like Bob Lemon did.

In the twenty-five years George Steinbrenner has owned the Yankees, fourteen different men have managed for the Boss. Some managed well; others couldn't take the heat they knew was coming when they signed the contract. In that quarter century, Steinbrenner has had an opinion on every manager he employed. He loved Billy Martin and respected Lou Piniella. Dallas Green was a mistake on both parts, and the Boss found out a little too late the warts on Buck Showalter's personality.

The Boss's opinion of Joe? "Number one, he is a man's man. He reminds me of a guy named Lou Saban. I was an assistant football coach at Northwestern with him," Steinbrenner said. "He was a man's man. [Torre] is the kind of guy who, if I was in a foxhole, I would want with me. I would like to have him standing in the trench with me."

Of course there have been managers—Green, for example—who firmly believed the Boss was the enemy. Helping the Torre-Steinbrenner relationship go as smoothly as it has is that Torre, though opinionated, is at the same time noncombative. He doesn't rant and rave when he has something to say, and he doesn't storm out of meetings when his suggestions fall on deaf ears.

"I enjoy it," Torre has said of his interactions with Steinbrenner. "Even when he isn't in such a good mood, I still enjoy being with him. I can talk to him. I've had two owners, one in St. Louis and one in Atlanta, that I didn't have access to. So if you have an idea or want to talk about something or get a point across, I can get it across."

Also working in Torre's favor is the fact that Steinbrenner isn't called the Boss just because it looks great on the back page of the *Post*.

"He is good enough to understand the chain of command. He understands who is the boss and is comfortable with it," Steinbrenner says. "When we talk, I will say something and he listens very good. Then he explains his opinion. Sometimes he says I'm right and sometimes he says I'm wrong."

When Steinbrenner listened to senior adviser Arthur Richman and tabbed Torre as Showalter's successor, he was flying blind. Richman, who knows everybody in baseball, pushed for Torre ahead of Steinbrenner's other suggestions, Tony LaRussa, Sparky Anderson, and Davey Johnson.

"I knew nothing about him other than he was a very good player and an experienced manager who had failed," the Boss recalled. "I got my [butt] roasted for hiring him. Everybody in New York gave it to me pretty good. I told Arthur to give me a list of four managers. Davey Johnson was on the list, and I have great affection for Davey Johnson, but Joe was

Arthur's first choice. I told him I knew I was going to get hurt on this, but Arthur didn't back off."

Maybe Torre's record reflected less his abilities as a manager than who he had playing for him. For the first time in his managerial career, Torre had the talent.

"Being a coach, I knew you could just do so much with X's and O's. If you don't have the horses, you can't be a good coach," Steinbrenner said. "When we were coaching at Northwestern, we were the same coaches. But when we went to Purdue and they had Len Dawson and Lamar Lundy, we had the horses."

Of course, there have been differences between Torre and Steinbrenner, but nothing near the battles Billy Martin used to wage against the Boss, or the cold war that highlighted the Green era. Torre was blindsided by the Boss downloading Mariano Duncan from the second base equation in 1997, and the Boss didn't appreciate Torre conceding the A.L. East to the Orioles before the Yankees were mathematically eliminated in the same season.

"God knows I have had enough [managers]," Steinbrenner said of the Brooklyn native. "I have a lot of respect for the man, and that's as nice a thing as I can say about anybody. The bottom line is that he is a New Yorker, and that means a lot to me."

As for Zimmer, well, he's a treasure the game will never replace.

Sinatra's voice working through the haze of a saloon. Bogey telling a dame how it was going to be. The Yankees in the World Series. We don't set those sights and sounds up, but when they surface they make us feel comfortable. We don't know why, but they do.

Add Zimmer sitting in a dugout to the list.

It's nine A.M. on a Sunday, the Kauffman Stadium dew just about evaporated into a cloudless Kansas City sky, and Zimmer is perched on the bench looking out at another baseball morning.

Zimmer in a baseball uniform in a dugout. Was he born this way on January 1, 1931, in Cincinnati?

As a player with the Dodgers—in Brooklyn and L.A.—the Cubs, the Mets, the Reds, and the Senators. As a manager with the Padres, Red Sox, Rangers, and Cubs. As a coach with the Expos, Red Sox, Cubs, Giants, Rockies, and Yankees. Zimmer fits perfectly in a dugout.

From Cambridge in 1949 to Jackie Robinson to October 2, 1978, to Derek Jeter, there isn't much Zimmer hasn't seen. Now, in his fiftieth year in professional baseball, Zimmer hints that this could be it. No more mornings like this. No more jolts of juice escorted into his veins by the first pitch of a big league game. The stomach still tightens and the game means more to him than ever. But at sixty-seven, with twin grandsons involved in athletics at St. Petersburg High, Zimmer smells the finish line.

"I have always said the day I don't enjoy walking into the clubhouse and coming out here in this dugout, that's the day I will go home," said Zimmer, who did that in 1995 when he was Don Baylor's bench coach in Colorado, but accepted Joe Torre's offer to return to the bench in 1996.

So, how close is baseball to saying so long to a treasure the game can ill afford to lose?

"It might be this year. It wouldn't be so much not enjoying coming to this clubhouse, not enjoying being on this bench," Zimmer explained. "I get to see the twins play most of the football games but no baseball. Traveling, coming in here the other night at four A.M. and getting up at nine in the morning. I am sixty-seven years old; sometimes you get tired of that. Get up in an airplane and have that thing jumping all around, I say to myself, 'What am I doing here? Why aren't I at home on the boat dock in the backyard?' It's a combination of things."

And yet, the door remains open because of the man he sits next to: "The thing that helps keep me here is the man I am working for, Joe Torre. I didn't know him that well until I came here, but he is a very special person."

To a trainload of people, Zimmer has been more than special. Teammates love him and players thank him. As much as playing with Jackie Robinson, Pee Wee Reese, Johnny Podres, and Don Drysdale meant to him, and managing Andre Dawson, Ryne Sandberg, Jim Rice, and Fred Lynn were great thrills, Zimmer's voice catches a bit when he talks about the lesser lights who credit him for their careers.

"I have had players come to me and say, 'Skip, you made me a millionaire.' I tell them, 'No you made yourself a millionaire. I just happened to be the man who gave you the chance, you just took it and went with it,'" Zimmer said. "[Cleveland reliever] Paul Assenmacher, almost every time I see him, he says to me, 'You made me a millionaire.' Only because when I had him in Chicago, I put him in tough situations, and when he moved on, because of what he did in Chicago, he got up to a good salary.

"Heathcliff Slocumb, I took him to Chicago and put him in some tough situations. He makes two to three million dollars. Many a time he walks up to me to thank me. These are the things you can't put a price on."

Nor can you estimate the worth of a major league player's father thanking you.

"We got a guy in Chicago named Bob Scanlan. [General Manager] Jim Frey wanted to send Scanlan to the minors. I wanted to pitch him in Houston, and Frey wasn't too wild about it," Zimmer recalled. "Well, the seventh inning he is winning, 3–1, and has pitched his [butt] off. I am not going to let this guy lose it. So the minute he got somebody on, I went out and got him.

"Well, I have a letter at home from his daddy, it damn near makes me choke up. That's what it's all about."

Of course, the game has changed. What hasn't since 1949, when Zimmer hit .227 in seventy-one games for Cambridge?

"There are great players just like there were years ago. I think because of money and guaranteed contracts, a manager is reluctant to get on a player for not hustling or running a ball out. Number one, if he has a three-year contract and it's the first year of his contract, what are you going to do with him if he doesn't run a ball out? You can fine him, but is that the answer? If you sit him down, you are hurting yourself and the club, so that's not the answer. Years ago, if a guy didn't hustle or do what the manager said, it was pretty easy because you could send him to the minor leagues."

In a different era—and it's not Zimmer's era, because his fingerprints are all over several eras—the manager rarely had to worry about an attitude problem.

"Years ago, players got on other players so that the manager didn't have to do it," Zimmer said. "Very seldom today do you ever see a player criticize another player on a team for making a mental mistake or not hustling. It all has to come from either the manager or the coaches. When I went to the Dodgers, if I wasn't in the right place at the right time, Jackie Robinson or Pee Wee Reese would come up and tell me where the hell I should be, and that's the way it was."

Asking Zimmer to pick his best memory is a challenge for a man with memories for many lifetimes. As he leaned forward on the fungo bat and peered toward right field, Zimmer surprised with the answer.

"There are so many, but up until the time I went to Chicago"—and brilliantly guided the Cubs to the 1989 N.L. East title—"my biggest thrills all happened in the same day. That was in 1978. We [Red Sox] had a big lead, then blew a big lead, and then wound up winning the last eight games of the season to tie the Yankees.

"When I went to the ballpark on Monday morning for a

one-game playoff, you know it was going to take care of the whole season, that was a thrill walking into Fenway Park for that game. That was one of my biggest thrills at that time. The way the team played the last eight games."

For every thrill, the bottom has to fall out of the stomach. For Zimmer, October 2, 1978, was the ultimate roller coaster.

"The biggest disappointment was losing. Now if we got beat 8–1, it wouldn't have been the biggest disappointment because we would have gone out and gotten our rear end beat," Zimmer said, squinting with eyes that could have been seeing Bucky Dent's cheap pop fly homer climb over the most famous wall—the Green Monster—in the world at that very moment. "But we had the game won two or three times."

Taking the Cubs to the top removed most of the sting that Dent put in Zimmer's huge heart.

"That night we clinched in Montreal was my biggest thrill because it was the first time I had won," Zimmer said. "If I had won in Boston, it probably wouldn't have been as big a thrill because people picked us to win in Boston. Well, we took a team nobody picked to win and won."

Now, Zimmer is with a team that won two World Series in three years. When he looks back on the fifty years, he shakes a head that has a metal plate in it thanks to a minor league beaning.

"When you stop and think where I have been—not what I have done, but where I have been, and who I have met, and the fun I have had—how can anybody in the world top that?" Zimmer asked. "How could a guy have a better ride than me?"

Part 2

The Yankee Roster:
Season and Career Statistics*

*For active players

TORRE,
Joseph Paul (Joe)
#06, Manager

Height: 6'2"
Weight: 212
Born: 7/18/40 in Brooklyn, NY
Resides: Harrison, NY
Bats: Right
Throws: Right
Married: Alice
Children: Michael, Lauren, Tina, and Andrea Rae

Career Stats

YEAR	CLUB	POSITION	W	L
1977	METS	Sixth	49	68
1978	METS	Sixth	66	96
1979	METS	Sixth	63	99
1980	METS	Fifth	67	95
1981	METS	Fifth (1st half)	17	34
1981	METS	Fourth (2nd half)	24	28
1982	ATLANTA	First	89	73
1983	ATLANTA	Second	88	74
1984	ATLANTA	Second (tie)	80	82
1990	ST. LOUIS	Sixth	24	34
1991	ST. LOUIS	Second	84	78
1992	ST. LOUIS	Third	83	79
1993	ST. LOUIS	Third	87	75
1994	ST. LOUIS	Third(tie)	53	61
1995	ST. LOUIS	Fourth	20	27
1996	YANKEES	First	92	70
1997	YANKEES	Second	96	66
Major League Totals			1082	1139

BROSIUS,
Scott David
#18, 3B

Height: 6'1"
Weight: 202
Born: 8/15/66 in Hillsboro, OR
Resides: McMinnville, OR
Bats: Right
Throws: Right
Married: Jennifer
Children: Allison, Megan, and David

Regular Season Stats

AVG	G	AB	R	H
.302	151	527	86	159
2B	**3B**	**HR**	**RBI**	**BB**
34	0	19	98	52
SO	**SB**	**CS**	**SLG%**	**OBP%**
97	11	8	.474	.373

Career Stats

Year	Club	AVG	G	AB	R	H	2B	3B	HR	RBI	BB	SO	SB
1987	Medford	.286	65	255	34	73	18	1	3	49	26	36	5
1988	Madison	.304	132	504	82	153	28	2	9	58	56	67	13
1989	Huntsville	.271	128	461	68	125	22	2	7	60	58	62	4
1990	Huntsville	.296	142	547	94	162	39	2	23	88	81	81	12
	Tacoma	.143	3	7	2	1	0	1	0	0	1	3	0
1991	Tacoma	.286	65	245	28	70	16	3	8	31	18	29	4
	OAKLAND	.235	36	68	9	16	5	0	2	4	3	11	3
1992	Tacoma	.237	63	236	29	56	13	0	9	31	23	44	8
	OAKLAND	.218	38	87	13	19	2	0	4	13	3	13	3
1993	Tacoma	.297	56	209	38	62	13	2	8	41	21	50	8
	UAKLAND	.249	70	213	26	53	10	1	6	25	14	37	6
1994	OAKLAND	.238	96	324	31	77	14	1	14	49	24	57	2
1995	OAKLAND	.262	123	389	69	102	19	2	17	46	41	67	4
1996	Edmonton	.625	3	8	5	5	1	0	0	0	3	1	0
	OAKLAND	.304	114	428	73	130	25	0	22	71	59	85	7
1997	Modesto	.333	2	3	1	1	0	0	0	1	1	0	0
	OAKLAND	.203	129	479	59	97	20	1	11	41	34	102	9
	Minor League Totals	.286	659	2475	381	708	150	13	67	359	288	373	54
	Major League Totals	.248	606	1988	280	494	95	5	76	249	178	372	34

BUSH,
Homer Giles
#22, 2B

Height: 5'10"
Weight: 175
Born: 11/12/72 in East St. Louis, IL
Resides: East St. Louis, IL
Bats: Right
Throws: Right

Regular Season Stats

AVG	G	AB	R	H
.371	44	70	16	26
2B	**3B**	**HR**	**RBI**	**BB**
3	0	1	5	5
SO	**SB**	**CS**	**SLG%**	**OBP%**
19	6	3	.457	.413

Career Stats

YEAR	CLUB	AVG	G	AB	R	H	2B	3B	HR	RBI	BB	SO	SB
1991	Scottsdale	.323	32	127	16	41	3	2	0	16	4	33	11
1992	Charleston	.234	108	367	37	86	10	5	0	18	13	86	14
1993	Waterloo	+.322	130	472	63	+152	19	3	5	51	19	87	39
1994	Rancho Cucamonga	.335	39	161	37	54	10	3	0	16	9	29	9
	Wichita	.298	59	245	35	73	11	4	3	14	10	39	20
1995	Memphis	.280	108	432	53	121	12	5	5	37	15	83	34
1996	Las Vegas	.362	32	116	24	42	11	1	2	3	3	33	3
1997	Las Vegas	.277	38	155	25	43	10	1	3	14	7	40	5
	Columbus	.247	74	275	36	68	10	3	2	26	25	56	12
	YANKEES	.364	10	11	2	4	0	0	0	3	0	0	0
	Minor League Totals	.289	620	2350	326	680	96	27	20	195	105	485	147
	Major League Totals	.364	10	11	2	4	0	0	0	3	0	0	0

CONE, David
#36, RHP

Height: 6'1"
Weight: 190
Born: 1/2/63 in Kansas City, MO
Resides: New York, NY
Bats: Left
Throws: Right
Married: Lynn

Regular Season Stats

W	L	S	ERA
20	7	0	3.55
G	GS	CG	SHO
31	31	3	0
IP	H	R	ER
207.2	186	89	82
HR	BB	SO	
20	59	209	

Career Stats

YEAR	CLUB	W-L	ERA	G	GS	CG	Sho	SV	IP	H	R	ER	BB	SO
1981	Sarasota	6-4	2.55	14	12	0	0	0	67.0	52	24	19	33	45
1982	Charleston	9-2	2.06	16	16	1	1	0	105.0	84	38	24	47	87
	Ft. Meyers	7-1	2.12	10	9	6	1	0	72.0	56	21	17	25	57
1984	Memphis	8-12	4.27	29	29	9	1	0	179.0	162	103	85	111	114
1985	Omaha	9-15	4.65	28	27	5	1	0	158.2	157	90	82	+93	115
1986	Omaha	8-4	2.79	39	2	2	0	14	71.0	60	23	22	25	63
	KANSAS CITY	0-0	5.56	11	0	0	0	0	22.2	29	14	14	13	21
1987	Tidewater	0-1	5.73	3	3	0	0	0	11.0	10	8	7	6	7
	METS	5-6	3.71	21	13	1	0	1	99.1	87	46	41	44	68
1988	METS	20-3	2.22	35	28	8	4	0	231.1	178	67	57	80	213
1989	METS	14-8	3.52	34	33	7	2	0	219.2	183	92	86	74	190
1990	METS	14-10	3.23	31	30	6	2	0	211.2	177	84	76	65	+233
1991	METS	14-14	3.29	34	34	5	2	0	232.2	204	95	85	73	+241
1992	METS	13-7	2.88	27	27	7	5	0	196.2	162	75	63	82	214
	TORONTO	4-3	2.55	8	7	0	0	0	53.0	39	16	15	29	47
1993	KANSAS CITY	11-14	3.33	34	34	6	1	0	254.0	205	102	94	114	191
1994	KANSAS CITY	16-5	2.94	23	23	4	3	0	171.2	130	60	56	54	132
1995	TORONTO	9-6	3.38	17	17	5	2	0	130.1	113	53	49	41	102
	YANKEES	9-2	3.82	13	13	1	0	0	99.0	82	42	42	47	89
1996	Norwich	0-0	0.90	2	2	0	0	0	10.0	9	3	1	1	13
	YANKEES	7-2	2.88	11	11	1	0	0	72.0	50	25	23	34	71
1997	YANKEES	12-6	2.82	29	29	1	0	0	195.0	155	67	61	86	222
	Minor League Totals	47-39	3.43	141	100	23	4	14	673.2	590	310	257	341	501
	AL Totals	68-38	3.19	146	134	18	6	0	997.2	803	379	354	418	875
	NL Totals	80-48	3.08	182	165	34	15	1	1191.1	991	459	408	418	1159
	Major League Totals	148-86	3.13	328	299	52	21	1	2189.0	1794	838	762	836	2034

CURTIS,
Chad
#28, OF

Height: 5'10"
Weight: 185
Born: 11/6/68 in Marion, IN
Resides: Middleville, MI
Bats: Right
Throws: Right

Regular Season Stats

AVG	G	AB	R	H
.242	150	455	78	110
2B	3B	HR	RBI	BB
21	1	10	55	74
SO	SB	CS	SLG%	OBP%
80	21	4	.358	.352

Career Stats

YEAR	CLUB	AVG	G	AB	R	H	2B	3B	HR	RBI	BB	SO	SB
1989	Mesa	.303	32	122	30	37	4	4	3	20	14	20	17
	Quad City	.244	23	78	7	19	3	0	2	11	6	17	7
1990	Quad City	.307	135	+492	87	+151	28	1	14	65	57	76	64
1991	Edmonton	.316	115	431	81	136	28	7	9	61	52	58	46
1992	CALIFORNIA	.259	139	441	59	114	16	2	10	46	51	71	43
1993	CALIFORNIA	.285	152	583	94	166	25	3	6	59	70	89	48
1994	CALIFORNIA	.256	114	453	67	116	23	4	11	50	37	69	25
1995	DETROIT	.268	144	586	96	157	29	3	21	67	70	93	27
1996	DETROIT	.263	104	400	65	105	20	1	10	37	53	73	16
	LOS ANGELES	.212	43	104	20	22	5	0	2	9	17	15	2
1997	CLEVELAND	.207	22	29	8	6	1	0	3	5	7	10	0
	YANKEES	.291	93	320	51	93	21	1	12	50	36	49	12
	Minor League Totals	.305	305	1123	205	343	63	12	28	157	129	171	134
	AL Totals	.269	768	2812	440	757	135	14	73	314	324	454	171
	NL Totals	.212	43	104	20	22	5	0	2	9	17	15	2
	Major League Totals	.267	811	2916	460	779	140	14	75	323	341	469	173

DAVIS,
Chili
#20, DH/OF

Height: 6'3"
Weight: 217
Born: 1/17/60 in Kingston, Jamaica
Resides: Scottsdale, AZ
Bats: Both
Throws: Right
Children: Charles Theodore, Jr.

Regular Season Stats

AVG	G	AB	R	H
.294	34	102	10	30
2B	**3B**	**HR**	**RBI**	**BB**
7	0	3	9	13
SO	**SB**	**CS**	**SLG%**	**OBP%**
18	0	1	.451	.371

Career Stats

YEAR	CLUB	AVG	G	AB	R	H	2B	3B	HR	RBI	BB	SO	SB	CS
1981	SAN FRANCISCO	.133	8	15	1	2	0	0	0	0	1	2	2	0
1982	SAN FRANCISCO	.261	154	641	86	167	27	6	19	76	45	115	24	13
1983	SAN FRANCISCO	.233	137	486	54	113	21	2	11	59	55	108	10	12
1984	SAN FRANCISCO	.315	137	499	87	157	21	6	21	81	42	74	12	8
1985	SAN FRANCISCO	.270	136	481	53	130	25	2	13	56	62	74	15	7
1986	SAN FRANCISCO	.278	153	526	71	146	28	3	13	70	84	96	16	13
1987	SAN FRANCISCO	.250	149	500	80	125	22	1	24	76	72	109	16	9
1988	CALIFORNIA	.268	158	600	81	161	29	3	21	93	56	118	9	10
1989	CALIFORNIA	.271	154	560	81	152	24	1	22	90	61	109	3	0
1990	CALIFORNIA	.265	113	412	58	109	17	1	12	58	61	89	1	2
1991	MINNESOTA	.277	153	534	84	148	34	1	29	93	95	117	5	6
1992	MINNESOTA	.288	138	444	63	128	27	2	12	66	73	76	4	5
1993	CALIFORNIA	.243	152	573	74	139	32	0	27	112	71	135	4	1
1994	CALIFORNIA	.311	108	392	72	122	18	1	26	84	69	84	3	2
1995	CALIFORNIA	.318	119	424	81	135	23	0	20	86	89	79	3	3
1996	CALIFORNIA	.292	145	530	73	155	24	0	28	95	86	99	5	2
1997	KANSAS CITY	.279	140	477	71	133	20	0	30	90	85	96	6	3
Minor League Totals		.295	485	1734	292	511	90	20	70	319	218	351	109	
AL Totals		.279	1381	4946	738	1382	248	9	227	867	746	1002	43	
NL Totals		.267	874	3148	432	840	144	20	101	418	361	578	95	
Majorleague Totals		.275	2255	8094	1170	2222	392	29	328	1285	1107	1580	138	

GIRARDI,
Joseph Elliott
#25, C

Height: 5'11"
Weight: 195
Born: 10/14/64 in Peoria, IL
Resides: Lake Forest, IL
Bats: Right
Throws: Right
Married: Kim

Regular Season Stats

AVG	G	AB	R	H
.276	78	254	31	70
2B	**3B**	**HR**	**RBI**	**BB**
11	4	3	31	14
SO	**SB**	**CS**	**SLG%**	**OBP%**
38	2	4	.386	.317

Career Stats

YEAR	CLUB	AVG	G	AB	R	H	2B	3B	HR	RBI	BB	SO	SB
1986	Peoria	.309	68	230	36	71	13	1	3	28	17	36	6
1987	Winston–Salem	.280	99	364	51	102	9	8	8	46	33	64	9
1988	Pittsfield	.272	104	357	44	97	14	1	7	41	29	51	7
1989	CUBS	.248	59	157	15	39	10	0	1	14	11	26	2
	Iowa	.245	32	110	12	27	4	2	2	11	5	19	3
1990	CUBS	.270	133	419	36	113	24	2	1	38	17	50	8
1991	CUBS	.191	21	47	3	9	2	0	0	6	6	6	0
	Iowa	.222	12	36	3	8	1	0	0	4	4	8	2
1992	CUBS	.270	91	270	19	73	3	1	1	12	19	38	0
1993	COLORADO	.290	86	310	35	90	14	5	3	31	24	41	6
	Colorado Springs	.484	8	31	6	15	1	1	1	6	0	3	1
1994	COLORADO	.276	93	330	47	91	9	4	4	34	21	48	3
1995	COLORADO	.262	125	462	63	121	17	2	8	55	29	76	3
1996	YANKEES	.294	124	422	55	124	22	3	2	45	30	55	13
1997	YANKEES	.264	112	398	38	105	23	1	1	50	26	53	2
	Minor League Totals	.284	323	1128	152	320	42	13	21	136	88	181	28
	Major League Totals	.272	844	2815	311	765	124	18	21	285	183	393	37

HERNANDEZ, Orlando
#26, RHP

Height: 6'2"
Weight: 190
Born: 10/11/69 in Villa Clara, Cuba
Bats: Right
Throws: Right
Married: Norris Bosch

Regular Season Stats

W	L	S	ERA
12	4	0	3.13
G	**GS**	**CG**	**SHO**
21	21	3	1
IP	**H**	**R**	**ER**
141.0	113	53	49
HR	**BB**	**SO**	
11	52	131	

Career Stats

YEAR	CLUB	W–L	ERA	GS	IP	H	R	ER	BB	SO
1998	Tampa (A)	1–1	1.00	2	9.0	3	2	1	3	15
	Columbus (AAA)	6–0	3.83	7	42.1	41	19	18	17	59
	Minor League Totals	7–1	3.33	9	51.1	44	21	19	20	74

IRABU,
Hideki
#14, RHP

Height: 6'4"
Weight: 240
Born: 5/5/69 in Hyogo, Japan
Resides: Chiba, Japan
Bats: Right
Throws: Right
Married: Kyonsu

Regular Season Stats

W	L	S	ERA
13	9	0	4.00
G	**GS**	**CG**	**SHO**
28	28	2	1
IP	**H**	**R**	**ER**
171.0	144	77	76
HR	**BB**	**SO**	
27	76	123	

Career Stats

YEAR	CLUB	W–L	ERA	G	GS	CG	SHO	SV	IP	H	R	ER	BB	SO
1988	Lotte	2–5	3.69	14	6			1	39.1	30	19	17	15	21
1989	Lotte	0–2	3.53	33	2			9	51.0	37	20	20	27	50
1990	Lotte	8–5	3.78	34	7			0	123.2	110	56	52	72	102
1991	Lotte	3–8	6.88	24	14			0	100.2	110	78	77	70	78
1992	Chiba Lotte	0–5	3.86	28	4			0	77.0	78	38	33	37	55
1993	Chiba Lotte	8–7	3.10	32	8			1	142.1	125	59	49	58	160
1994	Chiba Lotte	+15–10	3.04	27	20			0	207.1	170	77	70	94	+239
1995	Chiba Lotte	11–11	+2.53	28	18			0	203.0	158	70	57	72	+239
1996	Chiba Lotte	12–6	+2.40	23	20			0	157.1	108	57	42	59	167
1997	Tampa (FSL)	1–0	0.00	2	2	0	0	0	9.0	4	0	0	0	12
	Norwich	1–1	4.50	2	2	0	0	0	10.0	13	5	5	0	9
	Columbus	2–0	1.67	4	4	1	1	0	27.0	19	7	5	5	28
	YANKEES	5–4	7.09	13	9	0	0	0	53.1	69	47	42	20	56
	Pacific League Totals	59–59	3.41	243	99			11	1101.2	926	475	417	504	1111
	Minor League Totals	4–1	1.96	8	8	1	1	0	46.0	36	12	10	5	49
	Major League Totals	5–4	7.09	13	9	0	0	0	53.1	69	47	42	20	56

JETER,
Derek
#2, SS

Height: 6'3"
Weight: 185
Born: 6/26/74 in Pequannock, NJ
Resides: Tampa, FL
Bats: Right
Throws: Right

Regular Season Stats

AVG	G	AB	R	H
.325	148	622	126	202
2B	**3B**	**HR**	**RBI**	**BB**
25	8	19	84	57
SO	**SB**	**CS**	**SLG%**	**OBP%**
118	30	6	.482	.384

Career Stats

YEAR	CLUB	AVG	G	AB	R	H	2B	3B	HR	RBI	BB	SO	SB
1992	Tampa	.202	47	173	19	35	10	0	3	25	19	36	2
	Greensboro	.243	11	37	4	9	0	0	1	4	7	16	0
1993	Greensboro	.295	128	515	85	152	14	11	5	71	58	95	18
1994	Tampa (FSL)	.329	69	292	61	96	13	8	0	39	23	30	28
	Albany	.377	34	122	17	46	7	2	2	13	15	16	12
	Columbus	.349	35	126	25	44	7	1	3	16	20	15	10
1995	Columbus	.317	123	486	96	154	27	9	2	45	61	56	20
	YANKEES	.250	15	48	5	12	4	1	0	7	3	11	0
1996	YANKEES	.314	157	582	104	183	25	6	10	78	48	102	14
1997	YANKEES	.291	159	654	116	190	31	7	10	70	74	125	23
	Minor League Totals	.306	447	1751	307	536	78	31	16	213	203	264	90
	Major League Totals	.300	331	1284	225	385	60	14	20	155	125	238	37

KNOBLAUCH, Chuck
#11, 2B

Height: 5'9"
Weight: 169
Born: 7/7/68 in Houston, TX
Resides: Houston, TX
Bats: Right
Throws: Right
Married: Lisa

Regular Season Stats

AVG	G	AB	R	H
.266	149	602	116	160
2B	**3B**	**HR**	**RBI**	**BB**
25	4	17	64	74
SO	**SB**	**CS**	**SLG%**	**OBP%**
70	30	12	.405	.359

Career Stats

Year	Team	AVG	G	AB	R	H	2B	3B	HR	RBI	BB	SO	SB
1989	Kenosha	.286	51	196	29	56	13	1	2	19	32	23	9
	Visalia	.364	18	77	20	28	10	0	0	21	6	11	4
1990	Orlando	.289	118	432	74	125	23	6	1	53	63	31	23
1991	MINNESOTA	.281	151	565	78	159	24	6	1	50	59	40	25
1992	MINNESOTA	.297	155	600	104	178	19	6	2	56	88	60	34
1993	MINNESOTA	.277	153	602	82	167	27	4	2	41	65	44	29
1994	MINNESOTA	.312	109	445	85	139	45	3	5	51	41	56	35
1995	MINNESOTA	.333	136	538	107	179	34	8	11	63	78	95	46
1996	MINNESOTA	.341	153	578	140	197	35	12	13	72	98	74	45
1997	MINNESOTA	.291	156	611	117	178	26	10	9	58	84	84	62
Minor League Totals		.296	187	705	123	209	46	7	3	93	101	65	36
Major League Totals		.304	1013	3939	713	1197	210	49	43	391	513	453	276

LEDEE,
Ricardo Alberto
#64, OF

Height: 6'1"
Weight: 160
Born: 11/22/73 in Ponce, Puerto Rico
Resides: Salinas, Puerto Rico
Bats: Left
Throws: Left

Regular Season Stats

AVG	G	AB	R	H
.244	41	78	13	19
2B	**3B**	**HR**	**RBI**	**BB**
5	2	1	12	7
SO	**SB**	**CS**	**SLG%**	**OBP%**
29	3	1	.397	.302

Career Stats

YEAR	CLUB	AVG	G	AB	R	H	2B	3B	HR	RBI	BB	SO	SB
1990	Tampa (GCL)	.108	19	37	5	4	2	0	0	1	6	18	2
1991	Tampa (GCL)	.267	47	165	22	44	6	2	0	18	22	40	3
1992	Tampa (GCL)	.229	52	179	25	41	9	2	2	23	24	47	1
1993	Oneonta	.255	52	192	32	49	7	6	8	20	25	46	7
1994	Greensboro	.250	134	484	87	121	23	9	22	71	91	126	10
1995	Greensboro	.269	89	335	65	90	16	6	14	49	51	66	10
1996	Norwich	.365	39	137	27	50	11	1	8	37	16	25	2
	Columbus	.282	96	358	79	101	22	6	21	64	44	95	6
1997	Tampa (R)	.333	7	21	3	7	1	0	0	2	2	4	0
	Columbus	.306	43	170	38	52	12	1	10	39	21	49	4
	Minor League Totals	.265	578	2078	383	559	109	33	85	324	302	517	45

LLOYD,
Graeme John
#27, LHP

Height: 6'7"
Weight: 234
Born: 4/9/67 in Geelong, Victoria, Australia
Resides: Gnarwarre, Australia
Bats: Left
Throws: Left

Regular Season Stats

W	L	S	ERA
3	0	0	1.72
G	**GS**	**CG**	**SHO**
49	0	0	0
IP	**H**	**R**	**ER**
36.2	25	10	7
HR	**BB**	**SO**	
3	6	20	

Career Stats

YEAR	CLUB	W–L	ERA	G	GS	CG	Sho	SV	IP	H	R	ER	BB	SO
1988	Myrtle Beach	3–2	3.62	41	0	0	0	2	60.0	71	33	24	30	43
1989	Dunedin	0–0	10.13	2	0	0	0	0	3.0	6	3	3	1	0
	Myrtle Beach	0–0	5.40	1	1	0	0	0	5.0	5	4	3	0	3
1990	Myrtle Beach	5–2	2.72	19	6	0	0	6	50.0	51	20	15	16	42
1991	Dunedin	2–5	2.24	50	0	0	0	24	60.0	54	17	15	25	39
	Knoxville	0–0	0.00	2	0	0	0	0	2.0	1	0	0	1	2
1992	Knoxville	4–8	1.96	49	7	1	0	14	92.0	79	30	20	25	65
1993	MILWAUKEE	3–4	2.83	55	0	0	0	0	63.2	64	24	20	13	31
1994	MILWAUKEE	2–3	5.17	43	0	0	0	3	47.0	49	29	27	16	31
1995	MILWAUKEE	0–5	4.50	33	0	0	0	4	32.0	28	16	16	8	13
1996	MILWAUKEE	2–4	2.82	52	0	0	0	0	51.0	49	19	16	17	24
	YANKEES	0–2	17.47	13	0	0	0	0	5.2	12	11	11	5	6
1997	YANKEES	1–1	3.31	46	0	0	0	1	49.0	55	24	18	20	26
	Minor League Totals	14–17	2.65	164	14	1	0	46	272.0	267	107	80	98	194
	Major League Totals	8–19	3.91	242	0	0	0	8	248.1	257	122	108	78	131

MARTINEZ,
Constantino (Tino)
#24, 1B

Height: 6'2"
Weight: 210
Born: 12/7/67 in Tampa, FL
Resides: Tampa, FL
Bats: Left
Throws: Right
Married: Marie
Children: Olivia, T.J., and Victoria

Regular Season Stats

AVG	G	AB	R	H
.282	141	529	92	149
2B	**3B**	**HR**	**RBI**	**BB**
33	1	28	123	61
SO	**SB**	**CS**	**SLG%**	**OBP%**
82	2	1	.507	.356

Career Stats

YEAR	CLUB	AVG	G	AB	R	H	2B	3B	HR	RBI	BB	SO	SB
1989	Williamsport	.257	+137	+509	51	131	29	2	13	64	59	54	7
1990	Calgary	.320	128	453	83	145	28	1	17	93	74	37	8
	SEATTLE	.221	24	68	4	15	4	0	0	5	9	9	0
1991	Calgary	.326	122	442	94	144	34	5	18	86	82	44	3
	SEATTLE	.205	36	112	11	23	2	0	4	9	11	24	0
1992	SEATTLE	.257	136	460	53	110	19	2	16	66	42	77	2
1993	SEATTLE	.265	109	408	48	108	25	1	17	60	45	56	0
1994	SEATTLE	.261	97	329	42	86	21	0	20	61	29	52	1
1995	SEATTLE	.293	141	519	92	152	35	3	31	111	62	91	0
1996	YANKEES	.292	155	595	82	174	28	0	25	117	68	85	2
1997	YANKEES	.298	150	594	96	176	31	2	44	141	75	75	3
	Minor League Totals	.299	387	1404	228	420	91	8	48	243	215	135	18
	Major League Totals	.276	856	3085	428	852	165	8	157	570	341	469	8

MENDOZA,
Ramiro
#55, RHP

Height: 6'2"
Weight: 154
Born: 6/15/72 in Los Santos, Panama
Resides: Los Santos, Panama
Bats: Right
Throws: Right

Regular Season Stats

W	L	S	ERA
10	2	1	3.25
G	**GS**	**CG**	**SHO**
41	14	1	1
IP	**H**	**R**	**ER**
130.1	131	50	47
HR	**BB**	**SO**	
9	30	56	

Career Stats

YEAR	CLUB	W–L	ERA	G	GS	CG	Sho	SV	IP	H	R	ER	BB	SO
1992	Santo Domingo	10–2	2.29	15	15	5	0	0	109.2	93	37	26	28	79
1993	Tampa (GCL)	4–5	2.79	15	9	0	0	1	67.2	59	26	21	7	61
	Greensboro	0–1	2.45	2	0	0	0	0	3.2	3	1	1	5	3
1994	Tampa (FSL)	12–6	3.01	22	21	1	0	0	134.1	133	54	45	35	110
1995	Norwich	5–6	3.21	19	19	2	1	0	89.2	87	39	32	33	68
	Columbus	1–0	2.57	2	2	0	0	0	14.0	10	4	4	2	13
1996	Columbus	6–2	2.51	15	15	0	0	0	97.0	96	30	27	19	61
	YANKEES	4–5	6.79	12	11	0	0	0	53.0	80	43	40	10	34
1997	Columbus	0–0	5.68	1	1	0	0	0	6.1	7	6	4	1	4
	YANKEES	0–6	4.24	39	15	0	0	2	133.2	157	67	63	28	82
	Minor League Totals	38–22	2.76	91	82	8	1	1	522.1	488	197	160	130	399
	Major League Totals	12–11	4.97	51	26	0	0	2	186.2	237	110	103	38	116

NELSON,
Jeff
#43, RHP

Height: 6'8"
Weight: 235
Born: 11/17/66 in Baltimore, MD
Resides: Issaquah, WA
Bats: Right
Throws: Right
Married: Colette
Children: Chandler Grace and Gabrielle Victoria

Regular Season Stats

W	L	S	ERA
5	3	3	3.79
G	**GS**	**CG**	**SHO**
45	0	0	0
IP	**H**	**R**	**ER**
40.1	44	18	17
HR	**BB**	**SO**	
1	22	35	

Career Stats

YEAR	CLUB	W–L	ERA	G	GS	CG	Sho	SV	IP	H	R	ER	BB	SO
1984	Great Falls	0–0	54.00	1	0	0	0	0	0.2	3	4	4	3	1
	Bradenton	0–0	1.35	9	0	0	0	0	13.1	6	3	2	6	7
1985	Bradenton	0–5	5.51	14	7	0	0	0	47.1	72	50	29	32	31
1986	Bakersfield	0–7	6.69	24	11	0	0	0	71.1	80	83	53	84	37
	Great Falls	0–0	13.50	3	0	0	0	0	2.0	5	3	3	3	1
1987	Salinas	3–7	5.74	17	16	1	0	0	80.0	80	61	51	71	43
1988	San Bernardino	8–9	5.54	27	27	1	1	0	149.1	163	115	92	91	94
1989	Williamsport	7–5	3.31	15	15	2	0	0	92.1	72	41	34	53	61
1990	Williamsport	1–4	6.44	10	10	0	0	0	43.1	65	35	31	18	14
	Peninsula	2–2	3.15	18	7	1	1	6	60.0	47	21	21	25	49
1991	Jacksonville	4–0	1.27	21	0	0	0	12	28.1	23	5	4	9	34
	Calgary	3–4	3.90	28	0	0	0	7	32.1	39	19	14	15	26
1992	Calgary	1–0	0.00	2	0	0	0	0	3.2	0	0	0	1	0
	SEATTLE	1–7	3.44	66	0	0	0	6	81.0	71	34	31	44	46
1993	Calgary	1–0	1.17	5	0	0	0	1	7.2	6	1	1	2	6
	SEATTLE	5–3	4.35	71	0	0	0	1	60.0	57	30	29	34	61
1994	SEATTLE	0–0	2.76	28	0	0	0	0	42.1	35	18	13	20	44
	Calgary	1–4	2.84	18	0	0	0	8	25.1	21	9	8	7	30
1995	SEATTLE	7–3	2.17	62	0	0	0	2	78.2	58	21	19	27	96
1996	YANKEES	4–4	4.36	73	0	0	0	2	74.1	75	38	36	36	91
1997	YANKEES	3–7	2.86	77	0	0	0	2	78.2	53	32	25	37	81
	Minor League Totals	31–47	4.75	212	93	5	2	34	657.0	682	450	347	420	434
	Major League Totals	20–24	3.32	377	0	0	0	13	415.0	349	173	153	198	419

O'NEILL,
Paul Andrew
#21, RF

Height: 6'4"
Weight: 215
Born: 2/25/63 in Columbus, OH
Resides: Cincinnati, OH
Bats: Left
Throws: Left
Married: Nevalee
Children: Andrew, Aaron, and Alexandra

Regular Season Stats

AVG	G	AB	R	H
.317	151	600	95	190
2B	**3B**	**HR**	**RBI**	**BB**
40	2	24	115	57
SO	**SB**	**CS**	**SLG%**	**OBP%**
103	15	1	.510	.372

Career Stats

YEAR	CLUB	AVG	G	AB	R	H	2B	3B	HR	RBI	BB	SO	SB
1981	Billings	.315	66	241	37	76	7	2	3	29	21	35	6
1982	Cedar Rapids	.272	116	386	50	105	19	2	8	71	21	79	12
1983	Tampa	.278	121	413	62	115	23	7	8	51	56	70	20
	Waterbury	.279	14	43	6	12	0	0	0	6	6	8	2
1984	Vermont	.265	134	475	70	126	31	5	16	76	52	72	29
1985	Denver	.305	+137	+509	63	+155	+32	3	7	74	28	73	5
	CINCINNATI	.333	5	12	1	4	1	0	0	1	0	2	0
1986	Denver	.254	55	193	20	49	9	2	5	27	9	28	1
	CINCINNATI	.000	3	2	0	0	0	0	0	0	1	1	0
1987	Nashville	.297	11	37	12	11	0	0	3	6	5	5	1
	CINCINNATI	.256	84	160	24	41	14	1	7	28	18	29	2
1988	CINCINNATI	.252	145	485	58	122	25	3	16	73	38	65	8
1989	Nashville	.333	4	12	1	4	0	0	0	0	3	1	1
	CINCINNATI	.276	117	428	49	118	24	2	15	74	46	64	20
1990	CINCINNATI	.270	145	503	59	136	28	0	16	78	53	103	13
1991	CINCINNATI	.256	152	532	71	136	36	0	28	91	73	107	12
1992	CINCINNATI	.246	148	496	59	122	19	1	14	66	77	85	6
1993	YANKEES	.311	141	498	71	155	34	1	20	75	44	69	2
1994	YANKEES	+.359	103	368	68	132	25	1	21	83	72	56	5
1995	YANKEES	.300	127	460	82	138	30	4	22	96	71	76	1
1996	YANKEES	.302	150	546	89	165	35	1	19	91	102	76	0
1997	YANKEES	.324	149	553	89	179	42	0	21	117	75	92	10
	Minor League Totals	.283	658	2309	321	653	121	21	50	340	201	371	77
	AL Totals	.315	670	2425	399	769	166	7	103	462	364	369	18
	NL Totals	.259	799	2618	321	679	147	7	96	411	306	456	61
	Major League Totals	.287	1469	5043	720	1448	313	14	199	873	670	825	79

PETTITTE,
Andrew Eugene
#46, LHP

Height: 6'5"
Weight: 235
Born: 6/15/72 in Baton Rouge, LA
Resides: Deer Park, TX
Bats: Left
Throws: Left
Married: Laura
Children: Joshua Blake

Regular Season Stats

W	L	S	ERA
16	11	0	4.24
G	**GS**	**CG**	**SHO**
33	32	5	0
IP	**H**	**R**	**ER**
216.1	226	110	102
HR	**BB**	**SO**	
20	87	146	

Career Stats

YEAR	CLUB	W-L	ERA	G	GS	CG	Sho	SV	IP	H	R	ER	BB	SO
1991	Tampa	4-1	0.98	6	6	0	0	0	36.2	16	6	4	8	51
	Oneonta	2-2	2.18	6	6	1	0	0	33.0	33	18	8	16	32
1992	Greensboro	10-4	2.20	27	27	2	1	0	168.0	141	53	41	55	130
1993	Prince William	11-9	3.04	26	26	2	1	0	159.2	146	68	54	47	129
	Albany	1-0	3.60	1	1	0	0	0	5.0	5	4	2	2	6
1994	Albany	7-2	2.71	11	11	0	0	0	73.0	60	32	22	18	50
	Columbus	7-2	2.98	16	16	3	0	0	96.2	101	40	32	21	61
1995	YANKEES	12-9	4.17	31	26	3	0	0	175.0	183	86	81	63	114
	Columbus	0-0	0.00	2	2	0	0	0	11.2	7	0	0	0	8
1996	YANKEES	21-8	3.87	35	34	2	0	0	221.0	229	105	95	72	162
1997	YANKEES	18-7	2.88	35	35	4	1	0	240.1	233	86	77	65	166
	Minor League Totals	42-20	2.51	95	95	8	2	0	583.2	509	221	163	167	467
	Major League Totals	51-24	3.58	101	95	9	1	0	636.1	645	277	253	200	442

POSADA,
Jorge
#22, C

Height: 6'2"
Weight: 205
Born: 8/17/71 in Santurce, Puerto Rico
Resides: Rio Piedras, Puerto Rico
Bats: Both
Throws: Right

Regular Season Stats

AVG	G	AB	R	H
.271	110	354	56	96
2B	**3B**	**HR**	**RBI**	**BB**
23	0	17	63	47
SO	**SB**	**CS**	**SLG%**	**OBP%**
90	0	1	.480	.353

Career Stats

YEAR	CLUB	AVG	G	AB	R	H	2B	3B	HR	RBI	BB	SO	SB
1991	Oneonta	.235	71	217	34	51	5	5	4	33	51	51	6
1992	Greensboro	.277	101	339	59	94	22	4	12	58	58	87	11
1993	Prince William	.259	118	410	71	106	27	2	17	61	67	90	17
	Albany	.280	7	25	3	7	0	0	0	0	2	7	0
1994	Columbus	.240	92	313	46	75	13	3	11	48	32	81	5
1995	Columbus	.255	108	368	60	94	32	5	8	51	54	101	4
	YANKEES	.000	1	0	0	0	0	0	0	0	0	0	0
1996	Columbus	.271	106	354	76	96	22	6	11	62	79	86	3
	YANKEES	.071	8	14	1	1	0	0	0	0	1	6	0
1997	YANKEES	.250	60	188	29	47	12	0	6	25	30	33	1
	Minor League Totals	.258	603	2026	349	523	121	25	63	313	343	503	46
	Major League Totals	.238	69	202	30	48	12	0	6	25	31	39	1

RAINES,
Tim
#31, OF

Height: 5'8"
Weight: 186
Born: 9/16/59 in Sanford, FL
Resides: Heathrow, FL
Bats: Both
Throws: Right
Married: Virginia
Children: Tim, Jr. and Andre Darrel

Regular Season Stats

AVG	G	AB	R	H
.290	109	321	53	93
2B	**3B**	**HR**	**RBI**	**BB**
13	1	5	47	55
SO	**SB**	**CS**	**SLG%**	**OBP%**
49	8	3	.383	.395

Career Stats

YEAR	CLUB	AVG	G	AB	R	H	2B	3B	HR	RBI	BB	SO	SB
1977	Sarasota	.280	49	161	28	45	6	3	0	21	27	16	29
1978	W.Palm Beach	.287	100	359	67	103	10	0	0	23	64	44	57
1979	Memphis	.290	+145	+522	+104	160	25	10	5	50	90	51	59
	MONTREAL	.000	6	0	3	0	0	0	0	0	0	0	2
1980	Denver	+.354	108	429	105	152	23	#11	6	64	61	42	+77
	MONTREAL	.050	15	20	5	1	0	0	0	0	6	3	5
1981	MONTREAL	.304	88	313	61	95	13	7	5	37	45	31	+71
1982	MONTREAL	.277	156	647	90	179	32	8	4	43	75	83	+78
1983	MONTREAL	.298	156	615	+133	183	32	8	11	71	97	70	+90
1984	MONTREAL	.309	160	622	106	192	#38	9	8	60	87	69	+75
1985	MONTREAL	.320	150	575	115	184	30	13	11	41	81	60	70
1986	MONTREAL	+.334	151	580	91	194	35	10	9	62	78	60	70
1987	MONTREAL	.330	139	530	+123	175	34	8	18	68	90	52	50
1988	MONTREAL	.270	109	429	66	116	19	7	12	48	53	44	33
1989	MONTREAL	.286	145	517	76	148	29	6	9	60	93	48	41
1990	MONTREAL	.287	130	457	65	131	11	5	9	62	70	43	49
1991	WHITE SOX	.268	155	609	102	163	20	6	5	50	83	68	51
1992	WHITE SOX	.294	144	551	102	162	22	9	7	54	81	48	45
1993	WHITE SOX	.306	115	415	75	127	16	4	16	54	64	35	21
	Nashville	.455	3	11	3	5	1	0	0	2	2	0	2
1994	WHITE SOX	.266	101	384	80	102	15	5	10	52	61	43	13
1995	WHITE SOX	.285	133	502	81	143	25	4	12	67	70	52	13
1996	Tampa (GCL)	.600	1	5	2	3	2	0	0	3	1	0	0
	Tampa (FSL)	.361	9	36	9	13	2	0	2	11	8	3	0
	Norwich	.185	8	27	8	5	1	0	1	1	9	2	1
	Columbus	.250	4	12	3	3	1	0	0	0	1	3	1
	YANKEES	.284	59	201	45	57	10	0	9	33	34	29	10
1997	Tampa (GCL)	.250	1	4	0	1	0	0	0	2	1	1	0
	Tampa (FSL)	.343	11	35	8	12	0	0	2	5	11	1	1
	Norwich	.286	2	7	0	2	1	0	0	2	0	2	0
	Columbus	.154	4	13	1	2	0	0	0	0	3	2	0
	YANKEES	.321	74	271	56	87	20	2	4	38	41	34	8
	Minor League Totals	.312	445	1621	338	506	72	23	16	184	278	167	227
	AL Totals	.287	781	2933	541	841	128	30	63	448	434	309	161
	NL Totals	.301	1405	5305	934	1598	273	81	96	452	775	563	634
	Major League Totals	.296	2186	8238	1475	2439	401	111	159	900	1209	872	795

RIVERA,
Mariano
#42, RHP

Height: 6'2"
Weight: 168
Born: 11/29/69 in Panama City, Panama
Resides: La Chorrera, Panama
Bats: Right
Throws: Right

Regular Season Stats

W	L	S	ERA
3	0	36	1.91
G	**GS**	**CG**	**• SHO**
54	0	0	0
IP	**H**	**R**	**ER**
61.1	48	13	13
HR	**BB**	**SO**	
3	17	36	

Career Stats

YEAR	CLUB	W-L	ERA	G	GS	CG	SHO	SV	IP	H	R	ER	BB	SO
1990	Tampa	5–1	+0.17	22	1	1	1	1	52.0	17	3	1	7	58
1991	Greensboro	4–9	2.75	29	15	1	0	0	114.2	103	48	35	36	123
1992	Ft. Lauderdale	5–3	2.28	10	10	3	1	0	59.1	40	17	15	5	42
1993	Greensboro	1–0	2.06	10	10	0	0	0	39.1	31	12	9	15	32
	Tampa	0–1	2.25	2	2	0	0	0	4.0	2	1	1	1	6
1994	Columbus	4–2	5.81	6	6	1	0	0	31.0	34	22	20	10	23
	Albany	3–0	2.27	9	9	0	0	0	63.1	58	20	16	8	39
	Tampa (FSL)	3–0	2.21	7	7	0	0	0	36.2	34	12	9	12	27
1995	YANKEES	5–3	5.51	19	10	0	0	0	67.0	71	43	41	30	51
	Columbus	2–2	2.10	7	7	1	0	0	30.0	25	10	7	3	30
1996	YANKEES	8–3	2.09	61	0	0	0	5	107.2	73	25	25	34	130
1997	YANKEES	6–4	1.88	66	0	0	0	43	71.2	65	17	15	20	68
	Minor League Totals	27–18	2.38	102	67	7	2	1	430.1	344	145	113	97	380
	Major League Totals	19–10	2.96	146	10	0	0	48	246.1	209	85	81	84	249

SOJO,
Luis
#19, INF

Height: 5'11"
Weight: 175
Born: 1/3/66 in Barquisimeto, VZ
Resides: Barquisimeto, VZ
Bats: Right
Throws: Right
Married: Zulima
Children: LesLuis

Regular Season Stats

AVG	G	AB	R	H
.228	53	145	15	33
2B	**3B**	**HR**	**RBI**	**BB**
3	1	0	13	4
SO	**SB**	**CS**	**SLG%**	**OBP%**
15	1	0	.262	.247

Career Stats

YEAR	CLUB	AVG	G	AB	R	H	2B	3B	HR	RBI	BB	SO	SB
1987	Myrtle Beach	.211	72	223	23	47	5	4	2	15	17	18	5
1988	Myrtle Beach	.289	135	+536	83	+155	22	5	5	56	35	35	14
1989	Syracuse	.276	121	482	54	133	20	5	3	54	21	42	9
1990	Syracuse	.296	75	297	38	88	12	3	6	25	14	23	10
	TORONTO	.225	33	80	14	18	3	0	1	9	5	5	1
1991	CALIFORNIA	.258	113	364	38	94	14	1	3	20	14	26	4
1992	Edmonton	.297	37	145	22	43	9	1	1	24	9	17	4
	CALIFORNIA	.272	106	368	37	100	12	3	7	43	14	24	7
1993	Syracuse	.218	43	142	17	31	7	2	1	12	8	12	2
	TORONTO	.170	19	47	5	8	2	0	0	6	4	2	0
1994	Calgary	.324	24	102	19	33	9	3	1	18	10	7	5
	SEATTLE	.277	63	213	32	59	9	2	6	22	8	25	2
1995	SEATTLE	.289	102	339	50	98	18	2	7	39	23	19	4
1996	SEATTLE	.211	77	247	20	52	8	1	1	16	10	13	2
	YANKEES	.275	18	40	3	11	2	0	0	5	1	4	0
1997	YANKEES	.307	77	215	27	66	6	1	2	25	16	14	3
	Minor League Totals	.275	507	1927	256	530	84	23	19	204	114	154	49
	Major League Totals	.265	608	1913	226	506	74	10	27	185	95	132	23

SPENCER,
Michael Shane (Shane)
#68, OF

Height: 5'11"
Weight: 210
Born: 2/20/72 in Key West, FL
Resides: El Cajon, CA
Bats: Right
Throws: Right

Regular Season Stats

AVG	G	AB	R	H
.381	26	63	17	24
2B	**3B**	**HR**	**RBI**	**BB**
6	0	9	23	5
SO	**SB**	**CS**	**SLG%**	**OBP%**
11	0	1	.905	.420

Career Stats

YEAR	CLUB	AVG	G	AB	R	H	2B	3B	HR	RBI	BB	SO	SB
1990	Tampa (GCL)	.184	42	147	20	27	4	0	0	7	20	23	11
1991	Tampa (GCL)	.306	41	160	25	49	7	0	0	30	14	19	9
	Oneonta	.245	18	53	10	13	2	1	0	3	10	9	2
1992	Greensboro	.287	83	258	43	74	10	2	3	27	33	37	8
1993	Greensboro	.269	122	431	89	116	35	2	12	80	52	62	14
1994	Tampa (FSL)	.290	90	334	44	97	22	3	8	53	30	53	5
1995	Tampa (FSL)	.300	134	500	87	150	31	3	16	88	61	60	14
1996	Norwich	.253	126	450	70	114	19	0	29	89	68	99	4
	Columbus	.355	9	31	7	11	4	0	3	6	5	5	0
1997	Columbus	.241	125	452	78	109	34	4	30	86	71	105	0
Minor League Totals		.270	790	2816	473	760	168	15	101	469	364	472	66

STANTON,
Michael William (Mike)
#29, LHP

Height: 6'1"
Weight: 215
Born: 6/2/67 in Houston, TX
Resides: Houston, TX
Bats: Left
Throws: Left
Married: Debbie
Children: William, Michael , Karli Marie, Mitchell,
and Cameron

Regular Season Stats

W	L	S	ERA
4	1	6	5.47
G	**GS**	**CG**	**SHO**
67	0	0	0
IP	**H**	**R**	**ER**
79.0	71	51	48
HR	**BB**	**SO**	
13	26	69	

Career Stats

YEAR	CLUB	W–L	ERA	G	GS	CG	Sho	SV	IP	H	R	ER	BB	SO
1987	Pulaski	4–8	3.24	15	13	3	2	0	83.1	64	37	30	42	82
1988	Burlington	11–5	3.62	30	23	1	1	0	154.0	154	86	62	69	160
	Durham	1–0	1.46	2	2	1	1	0	12.1	14	3	2	5	14
1989	Greenville	4–1	1.58	47	0	0	0	19	51.1	32	10	9	31	54
	Richmond	2–0	0.00	13	0	0	0	8	20.0	6	0	0	13	20
	ATLANTA	0–1	1.50	20	0	0	0	7	24.0	17	4	4	8	27
1990	Greenville	0–1	1.59	4	4	0	0	0	5.2	7	1	1	3	7
	ATLANTA	0–3	18.00	7	0	0	0	2	7.0	16	16	14	4	7
1991	ATLANTA	5–5	2.88	74	0	0	0	7	78.0	62	27	25	21	54
1992	ATLANTA	5–4	4.10	65	0	0	0	8	63.2	59	32	29	20	44
1993	ATLANTA	4–6	4.67	63	0	0	0	27	52.0	51	35	27	29	43
1994	ATLANTA	3–1	3.55	49	0	0	0	3	45.2	41	18	18	26	35
1995	ATLANTA	1–1	5.59	26	0	0	0	1	19.1	31	14	12	6	13
	BOSTON	1–0	3.00	22	0	0	0	0	21.0	17	9	7	8	10
1996	BOSTON	4–3	3.83	59	0	0	0	1	56.1	58	24	24	23	46
	TEXAS	0–1	3.22	22	0	0	0	0	22.1	20	8	8	4	14
1997	YANKEES	6–1	2.57	64	0	0	0	3	66.2	50	19	19	34	70
	Minor League Totals	22–15	2.87	111	42	5	4	34	326.2	277	137	104	163	337
	AL Totals	11–5	3.14	167	0	0	0	4	166.1	145	60	58	69	140
	NL Totals	18–21	4.01	304	0	0	0	55	289.2	277	146	129	114	223
	Major League Totals	29–26	3.69	471	0	0	0	59	456.0	422	206	187	183	363

WELLS,
David
#33, LHP

Height: 6'4"
Weight: 225
Born: 5/20/63 in Torrance, CA
Resides: Palm Harbor, FL
Bats: Left
Throws: Left
Children: Brandon

Regular Season Stats

W	L	S	ERA
18	4	0	3.49
G	**GS**	**CG**	**SHO**
30	30	8	5
IP	**H**	**R**	**ER**
214.1	195	86	83
HR	**BB**	**SO**	
29	29	163	

Career Stats

YEAR	CLUB	W-L	ERA	G	GS	CG	Sho	SV	IP	H	R	ER	BB	SO
1982	Medicine-Hat	4-3	5.18	12	12	1	0	0	64.1	71	42	37	32	53
1983	Kinston	6-5	3.73	25	25	5	0	0	157.0	141	81	65	71	115
1984	Kinston	1-6	4.71	7	7	0	0	0	42.0	51	29	22	19	44
	Knoxville	3-2	2.59	8	8	3	1	0	59.0	58	22	17	17	34
1985	Syracuse						Did not play							
1986	Florence	0-0	3.55	4	1	0	0	0	12.2	7	6	5	9	14
	Ventura	2-1	1.89	5	2	0	0	0	19.0	13	5	4	4	26
	Knoxville	1-3	4.05	10	7	1	0	0	40.0	42	24	18	18	32
	Syracuse	0-1	9.82	3	0	0	0	0	3.2	6	4	4	1	2
1987	Syracuse	4-6	3.87	43	12	0	0	6	109.1	102	49	47	32	106
	TORONTO	4-3	3.99	18	2	0	0	1	29.1	31	14	13	12	32
1988	Syracuse	0-0	0.00	6	0	0	0	3	5.2	7	1	0	2	8
	TORONTO	3-5	4.62	41	0	0	0	4	64.1	65	36	33	31	56
1989	TORONTO	7-4	2.40	54	0	0	0	2	86.1	66	25	23	28	78
1990	TORONTO	11-6	3.14	43	25	0	0	3	189.0	165	72	66	45	115
1991	TORONTO	15-10	3.72	40	28	2	0	1	198.1	188	88	81	49	106
1992	TORONTO	7-9	5.40	41	14	0	0	2	120.0	138	84	72	36	62
1993	DETROIT	11-9	4.19	32	30	0	0	0	187.0	183	93	87	42	139
1994	Lakeland	0-0	0.00	2	2	0	0	0	6.0	5	0	0	0	3
	DETROIT	5-7	3.96	16	16	5	1	0	111.1	113	54	49	24	71
1995	DETROIT	10-3	3.04	18	18	3	0	0	130.1	120	54	44	37	83
	CINCINNATI	6-5	3.59	11	11	3	0	0	72.2	74	34	29	16	50
1996	BALTIMORE	11-14	5.14	34	34	3	0	0	224.1	247	132	128	51	130
1997	YANKEES	16-10	4.21	32	32	5	2	0	218.0	239	109	102	45	156
	Minor League Totals	21-30	3.80	125	76	10	1	9	518.2	503	263	219	205	437
	AL Totals	100-80	4.04	369	199	18	3	13	1558.1	1561	761	699	400	1028
	NL Totals	6-5	3.59	11	11	3	0	0	72.2	74	34	29	16	50
	Major League Totals	106-85	4.02	380	210	21	3	13	1631.0	1635	795	728	416	1078

WILLIAMS,
Bernabe Figueroa (Bernie)
#51, CF

Height: 6'2"
Weight: 205
Born: 9/13/68 in San Juan, Puerto Rico
Resides: Bayamon, Puerto Rico
Bats: Both
Throws: Right
Married: Waleska
Children: Bernie Alexander, Beatrice Noemi, and
Bianca

Regular Season Stats

AVG	G	AB	R	H
.336	127	497	100	167
2B	**3B**	**HR**	**RBI**	**BB**
30	5	26	96	74
SO	**SB**	**CS**	**SLG%**	**OBP%**
81	15	9	.573	.421

Career Stats

YEAR	CLUB	AVG	G	AB	R	H	2B	3B	HR	RBI	BB	SO	SB
1986	Sarasota	.270	61	230	+45	62	5	3	2	25	39	40	33
1987	Ft. Lauderdale	.155	25	71	11	11	3	0	0	4	18	22	9
	Oneonta	.344	25	93	13	32	4	0	0	15	10	14	9
1988	Prince William	+.335	92	337	72	113	16	7	7	45	65	65	29
1989	Albany	.252	91	314	63	79	11	8	11	42	60	72	26
	Columbus	.216	50	162	21	35	8	1	2	16	25	38	11
1990	Albany	.281	134	466	+91	131	28	5	8	54	+98	97	+39
1991	Columbus	.294	78	306	52	90	14	6	8	37	38	43	9
	YANKEES	.238	85	320	43	76	19	4	3	34	40	57	10
1992	Columbus	.306	95	363	68	111	23	9	8	50	52	61	20
	YANKEES	.280	62	261	39	73	14	2	5	26	29	36	7
1993	YANKEES	.268	139	567	67	152	31	4	12	68	53	106	9
1994	YANKEES	.289	108	408	80	118	29	1	12	57	61	54	16
1995	YANKEES	.307	144	563	93	173	29	9	18	82	75	98	8
1996	YANKEES	.305	143	551	108	168	26	7	29	102	82	72	17
1997	YANKEES	.328	129	509	107	167	35	6	21	100	73	80	15
	Minor League Totals	.284	651	2342	436	664	112	39	46	288	405	452	185
	Major League Totals	.292	810	3179	537	927	183	33	100	469	421	503	82

Part 3

The Yankees Win!
The Yankees Win! The 1998
Post-Season Playoffs and
the World Series

12

The Division Championship Series: One for the Straw

They had won an A.L. record 114 games, shattered the 1927 Yankee mark of 110 wins, the most in the fabled franchise's history, and were heavily favored to win their second World Series in three years.

Of course, they were confident. While all those wins meant nothing when David Wells threw the first pitch against the hard-hitting Rangers, it did breed a large amount of confidence. Still, in the back of their minds they knew what had happened a year earlier. Then, they were favored to beat the Indians in the best-of-five first-round series and lost in five. Now, they approached the Rangers with nervousness because they understood better than anybody that their wonderful season could end in a nanosecond.

For David Wells, that fine season was in the balance in the eighth inning of Game 1 with Rusty Greer at the plate. From the beginning, Wells handcuffed the muscular Rangers. But Todd Stottlemyre, the Rangers starter and son of Yankee pitching coach, Mel, was almost as effective. Now, with the menacing Juan Gonzalez on deck and Mark McLemore on second via a gift one-out double, Wells had to get Greer or leave a mess for Mariano Rivera to clean up. With a sold-out Yankee Stadium piercing a perfect Bronx night with raucous noise, the two-run bulge that Wells worked most of the game with was super model thin. And when Wells broke Greer's bat with a fastball on the hands that produced a dribbler toward Jeter, it looked like the lead's width was about to be reduced to dental floss.

"It's a do or die play, one you either make or don't make," said Jeter, who fielded the ball on the run with his glove and fired a seed to Tino Martinez to get Greer by a half a step. "If I don't make the play, Boomer is out of the game. I had to take a chance. It's a play I've made before."

But never in a bigger game. Buoyed by Jeter's sterling play and Wells's eight innings of hanging zeroes on the Rangers, the Yankees copped Game 1 of the A.L. Division Series 2–0, in front of 57,362. With a blazing fastball, Rivera worked a perfect ninth for the save.

"Derek's play was the play of the game and saved the game," said Wells, who improved to 5–0 in postseason action. Using 135 pitches, Wells allowed five hits, one walk, and struck out a postseason career-high nine.

Thanks to the Yankees being unable to put Stottlemyre away when they had the chance in the early innings, they needed Wells to pitch as well as he did. Playing in his first postseason game, Scott Brosius drove in Jorge Posada with the game's first run in the second with a ground single to right. Two mistakes on the double steal by catcher Ivan Rodriguez and second baseman

Mark McLemore allowed Chad Curtis to score the second run in the second and present Wells with a 2–0 cushion. Had Rodriguez pump-faked a throw to second where Brosius was headed, he would have caught Curtis coming home. Had McLemore charged Rodriguez's strong throw, he would have had a play on Curtis at the dish. As it turned out, Brosius was caught stealing but Curtis scored.

After watching Chuck Knoblauch get thrown out at home attempting to score from first on Paul O'Neill's first-inning double, the Yankees wasted Tino Martinez's leadoff double that Roberto Kelly's glove knocked down well above the right-center-field fence in the fourth.

From there, Stottlemyre matched Wells pitch for pitch.

"That was a classic one-on-one matchup," Joe Torre said. "David was running on fumes in the eighth, but he managed to get the outs he needed."

Wells's first challenge surfaced in the seventh when Mike Simms stepped in with two outs and two on. At 2–2, Wells went after Simms with a tantalizing change-up that Simms waved at for the final out.

In the eighth, Curtis got a bad jump on McLemore's one-out fly ball.

That had Torre pop out of the dugout in a full jog. Normally, Torre strolls to the mound and hooks the hurler. This time he wanted to know how Wells felt.

"I told him I was okay," Wells recalled, "and then Jorge said, 'He's got it, he has something left.'"

At 3–2, Wells caught Kelly looking. That left Greer, a .185 (5-for-27) hitter against Wells. Greer had singled off a diving Jeter's glove for the Rangers first hit in the fourth.

"Most shortstops eat the ball and don't throw it," Martinez said.

Then again, most shortstops aren't Jeter.

Greer went down on a slow roller to shortstop.

Instead of hitting with two on in the eighth, Gonzalez led off the ninth against Rivera and flied to left to complete an 0–for–4 night that put the A.L. West champions in a deeper-than-it-looked 1–0 hole.

Darryl Strawberry didn't play in Game 1, having undergone tests the day before to find out why his stomach hurt. And by the beginning of Game 2, Strawberry had undergone a CAT scan that found a growth on his colon. He was at home preparing for a colonoscopy the next day. Cancer was on everybody's mind, even if nobody wanted to acknowledge it. Yankee players did their best to try and think positively. Watching from his Philadelphia home, longtime friend Lenny Dykstra knew something was wrong with Strawberry when he didn't see him in uniform.

Against that scary backdrop, the Yankees turned to Andy Pettitte, a pitcher who had struggled late in the regular season, to get them a 2–0 lead.

Pettitte came through with a 3–1 victory that put them one win away from advancing, rewarding Joe Torre and Mel Stottlemyre for showing confidence in him while many were wondering if Torre had gone soft in the head for starting him. Pettitte was supported by a two-out solo homer from Shane Spencer in the second and a two-run homer by Scott Brosius in the fourth. Both dingers were hit off loser Rick Helling, a twenty-game winner, who, like Todd Stottlemyre the night before, deserved a better fate.

"The thing that motivated me the most was that I

wanted to have a great start for Skip [Torre] and Mel,"
said Pettitte, who allowed one run and three hits in
seven innings. He didn't issue a walk and fanned eight.
"They supported me when a lot of people were doubting
me. I was doubting myself a month ago."

Now, the Yankees were firmly in the driver's seat.
There was not one fleck of doubt in their universe. Of
course, there wasn't a shred of bravado either. There
were enough players in the clubhouse who remembered
winning the first two games against the Mariners in
1995, only to lose three straight in Seattle. This time, the
format called for a fifth game to be played at Yankee
Stadium if it was necessary. However, if the Rangers
could climb off the canvas to turn this into a one-game
deal, nearly everyone who'd been paying attention
would have been shocked.

In eighteen innings Yankee chuckers had limited the
best hitting team in the A.L. to one run and eleven hits.
Furthermore, the Bombers had been held to five runs
and won both games.

"What people forget is that we've won a lot of games
like this, with good pitching," Paul O'Neill said.

Yankee pitching had been better than good. Juan
Gonzalez, the A.L. leader in RBIs, went 1–for–4 and had
one hit in eight at-bats. Will Clark, who swung through
a 96-mph fastball from Mariano Rivera to end the second game, was 1–for–8. Ivan Rodriguez was 1–for–7.
As a team, a lineup that led the A.L. with a .289 batting
average was hitting an embarrassing .156.

The Yankees had so far checked in with a .246 mark.
Bernie Williams, Tino Martinez, and Chili Davis were a
combined 2–for–20 (.100) and hadn't driven in a run
yet. And the first five hitters were batting a combined

.121 (4–for–33). The difference in the series, clearly, had been the Yankees arms being better than those of the Rangers.

"In my opinion, playoff baseball is much like what you have seen," Rangers manager Johnny Oates said. "We have two of the most potent offensive teams in the American League and we've scored six runs in two games. I don't think we've swung the bats very well."

Pettitte didn't allow a base runner until Gonzalez led off the fifth with a double to left. He scored on Rodriguez's single and cut the Yankees' bulge to 3–1. Faced with his first test, Pettitte popped up Todd Zeile and got Mike Simms on a routine grounder to Brosius. Royce Clayton's two-out single off Jeff Nelson in the eighth forced Torre to summon Rivera from the pen. Armed with a lively fastball, Rivera ended the inning by getting Mark McLemore on a soft line drive to Chuck Knoblauch. Rivera gave up a leadoff single to Tom Goodwin in the ninth, but then overpowered Rusty Greer, Gonzalez, and Clark.

Wells one night, Pettitte the next, Rivera in both. All year long Torre had preached that the Yankees are all about pitching. Now they were about to pitch their way into the ALCS.

Strawberry didn't fly with the team to Texas after Game 2. And by the time most players arrived at the Ballpark in Arlington for an off-day workout, not many knew the dreaded news Torre would give them before practice started. Once they received word that Strawberry had cancer, their world was turned upside down.

No words were needed to understand their grief.

Watching the Yankees move from their clubhouse to a

runway that would carry them to the third base dugout, you knew the best team in baseball had been rocked from their caps to cleats. Minutes before, Torre had gathered the A.L. East champions and informed them that a malignant tumor was found on Strawberry's colon. Andy Pettitte and David Cone were a few of the Yankees who knew. Now, the rest of them heard it from a shaken Torre.

"There was complete silence," Torre recalled. "There was sobbing and some very sad people. When I talked to Darryl, I asked him how he was doing, and he told me they had found it was malignant. At that point, you don't know what the right thing to do is."

As they filed out of the clubhouse, the Bombers walked to the field somberly. Normally they're a loose group as they go through their pregame stretching routine. Now, they stretched in silence with eyes as empty as the seats they were staring at.

During a workout that included infield and batting practice, the only sound throughout the cavernous ballpark was that of balls hitting leather and wood. Otherwise, the Yankees went about getting ready for Game 3 of the A.L. Division Series against the Rangers in eerie silence.

"It was good that today was a workout day, we would have probably gotten our butts whipped if we played the game," Tino Martinez said. "He is a great guy and a popular guy on the team. That was probably the quietest workout we ever had."

The message Strawberry was sending from his North Jersey home was that his thoughts were with the Yankees as they tried to close out the Rangers that night.

"I have always said that this is a good man of great

character, and this has certainly proved that to be true,"
George Steinbrenner said. "He is facing a serious crisis,
and his concern is for his teammates. This is extremely
upsetting to me, and it really shows that baseball is only
a small part of life. Our thoughts and prayers are with
Darryl, his wife Charisse, and their young children."

"I talked to Darryl, not for long, but he told me how
proud he was to be part of this team," an emotional
Torre said. "It's tough, the only thing we can do is
pray."

And pray some more.

"We were in shock," said David Cone, who was on
the verge of tears several times. He was, after all, talking
about a teammate he watched develop into one of baseball's biggest stars before succumbing to the seductions
of booze and drugs, only to embrace sobriety and return
as a force at the plate.

"Everybody is concerned and worried. The fact that
Eric Davis has been through this will help. Darryl will
have a lot of confusion and will be scared. We're all
scared. He is a great human being."

Sober for four years, Strawberry had turned to God
to keep him away from temptation. So it was fitting that
Pettitte answered Strawberry's clubhouse call since Pettitte's religious convictions run very deep.

"I think I was the first one he let know that he had
cancer and that he would have surgery Saturday," Pettitte said. "It was tough. He wanted to let everybody
know he wasn't going to be with us and that he was
proud to be part of this team."

Torre has been involved in professional baseball since
1960, had a brother, Rocco, die in the middle of 1996 of
a heart attack, and went through the emotional roller

coaster of another brother, Frank, undergoing a heart transplant during the 1996 World Series.

"I had a tough one in '96," he said, "but this one whacked me as far as being blindsided. It ranks right there with one of the worst things I have had to deal with here."

Torre described Strawberry's mood as upbeat. So too did Pettitte. Eric Grossman, Strawberry's former agent and very close friend, said Strawberry's mood was positive since he was told the cancerous tumor was detected early.

That didn't surprise GM Brian Cashman.

"He's one of the strongest people I have ever met," Cashman said. "He's a fighter and he'll get through this."

The next night, the Yankees had to wait through a three hour sixteen minute rain delay before finishing off the Rangers with a 4–0 victory. David Cone pitched brilliantly, and Spencer, America's new baseball hero, homered along with Paul O'Neill.

Later they celebrated with champagne. It was a way of releasing the tension of having a sick teammate and surviving an always dangerous best-of-five series.

As the party wound down, Tim Raines got up on a table and made a toast to Strawberry. Suddenly, a chant of "Straw, Straw, Straw" filled the room.

If this was going to be a long October voyage, it was clear the Yankees weren't going to leave Strawberry behind.

Yankee Profile:
Darryl Strawberry

It's a shame it took colon cancer for America to understand that Darryl Strawberry was someone anybody would want their son to be. Sober for four-plus years, Strawberry had turned into a model citizen. Still, there were those who thought he was still the symbol of ballplayer greed, the home office for wasted talent.

On October 1, while the Yankees prepared to practice for Game 3 of the A.L. Division Series against the Rangers, Strawberry received the news nobody should ever have to hear: the two-month pain in his stomach was cancer and would require surgery. Suddenly, a nation's heart went out to a man who had beaten drugs and booze, and overcome a serious tax problem. His Yankee teammates and friends already knew what type of person Strawberry had turned into. Now, a country would find out because he was sick.

The alcohol and drugs altered Strawberry's personality. Too many times when he was high and drunk, Strawberry, perhaps the most talented hitter to grace the baseball landscape, was arrogant and believed the entire world was against him. It got to the point around the New York Mets in the hell-raising 1980s that teammates didn't look forward to long flights because sooner or later Strawberry was going to go off. One day he was fine, the next? Forget it. He stayed out far too late for a young player, was surly the next day, and asked out of the lineup too many times.

GM Frank Cashen, a man who had cut his baseball teeth in a different generation, turned his back on Strawberry after the 1990 season. Strawberry, fulfilling a longtime desire to play for the Dodgers with his friend, Eric Davis, signed as a free agent with Los Angeles. He was coming off a 37 homer, 108 RBI season, but the booze had extracted a toll on him. By the time he got to L.A., Strawberry was bothered by a bad back that would eventually require surgery and limit him to seventy-five games in 1992 and 1993.

A cocaine binge led to his release from the Dodgers at the beginning of the 1994 season. At the urging of Giants manager Dusty Baker, Strawberry hooked up with San Francisco on June 19. Following two weeks in the minors, Strawberry was back in the majors. With his brother, Michael, a former L.A. cop, assigned to keep an eye on him, the Giants had their fingers crossed that Strawberry could stay straight. But the seductive power of cocaine was too much for a man who, ironically, looked like he was put together off blueprints for the perfect body.

It wasn't until June 1995 that Strawberry made it back to the big leagues, signing with the Yankees. But manager Buck Showalter, like so many other baseball people who don't understand recovery, had little use for him. Showalter had heard all the horror stories and figured Strawberry was going to con him as well, and before long he was no longer a Yankee.

By the beginning of the 1996 season, Strawberry was playing for the St. Paul Saints of the Northern League, an outfit with no major league affiliation. After all those years, it had come to this: Darryl Strawberry was playing with a bunch of dreamers. The next Ted Williams was nowhere.

Meanwhile, in Yankeeland, Showalter no longer was in the

Yankee dugout. Instead, Joe Torre was running the show on the field, with Bob Watson in the GM's office. Neither were particularly hot for Strawberry, but George Steinbrenner loved reclamation projects, especially ones who had talent left. So, against Watson's wishes and without a ringing endorsement from Torre, the Boss treated himself to a Fourth of July birthday present by signing Strawberry. Two games for Columbus produced three homers in eight at-bats, and Strawberry was back in the big leagues, helping the Yankees win the A.L. East and the World Series.

The following season, 1997, was a waste. Due to a knee injury suffered in spring training but not operated on until June, Strawberry played in only eleven games. After a winter of rigorous workouts, he re-signed with the Yankees, agreeing to an incentive-laden contract that included a $2 million option for 1999. As usual, Strawberry reported to Tampa in 1998 looking like a Greek god, not an ounce of body fat on his body. He ran the bases well and looked good in the outfield.

"This time I'm going to stay healthy down here," he said. "You don't have to worry about that."

Strawberry played so well that, at the end of camp, Torre said he would be getting the majority of playing time in left, platooning with Chad Curtis and Tim Raines. Chili Davis, who was supposed to be the permanent DH, got hurt and changed the plan a bit, but there was no doubt the best baseball story of April was that of Darryl Strawberry. And possibly the biggest hit of the Yankees season was delivered by him on April 7.

On the night of April 6, Jamie Moyer had beaten the Yankees 8–0 to lower the Yanks record to 1–4. Prior to the next game, the Yankees held a meeting in which Joe Torre asked his club to be more aggressive. That translated into Chuck Knoblauch opening with a homer. Strawberry capped off a six-run inning with a two-run homer to dead-center off Jim Bullinger. Suddenly, the Yankees had air to breathe. Strawberry hit another homer, to center in the fourth, and finished the night with four RBIs. By the end of April, Strawberry was hitting .352 with six homers and fourteen RBIs in 54 at-bats.

In New York, a city with more baseball history than any other, Strawberry's story ranks right near the top. Young Met stud, almost swallowed by the sirens of the night, rebounds to be a Yankee force with a majestic swing booze and drugs couldn't destroy. The journey had been an arduous one, but now that Strawberry was back on top of the baseball heap, he pointed to Goldklang and Scott of the St. Paul Saints as two of the main reasons.

Would he have made it back to the big leagues if he hadn't been given a chance to display his skills in the independent Northern League? "Probably not," Strawberry answered. Major league teams had all but blackballed him in 1996, one year after he appeared in thirty-two games for the Yankees. "There is no way of knowing for sure, but going there and playing, I showed I still had enough left and that I had the desire. That was the most important thing."

Playing at St. Paul's Midway Stadium for $2,500 a month seemed light-years from what Strawberry was used to. But he was focused, hitting .435 with 18 homers and 39 RBIs in twenty-nine games. By July 7 he was in the Bronx.

"I saw him at Yankee Stadium before the home opener," said Goldklang, the Saints owner and a limited partner of George Steinbrenner's. "He said, 'Thank you, man.' There are a lot of people who receive help or that you help along the way. At some point, they forget who helped them. Darryl is a person who hasn't forgotten."

Scott, a former farm director of the Texas Rangers, saw Strawberry play in the Texas League (Double A) in 1982 but had never met or spoken to him until he contacted Strawberry about playing for St. Paul.

"I had mixed feelings about him," Scott recalled. "Talent-wise, we thought he could still play, but was he the new person he said he was? We took a lot of heat about it and we talked to Darryl several times. Finally I told him, 'If you're the person you say you are, we're going to get along great. If not, you aren't going to be a headache for the St. Paul Saints or Marty Scott, you're going to be a problem for one day.' Now I'm sorry I ever said that because from day one, he's been a class act."

And a very dear friend to Scott and his family.

"Our personal relationship didn't develop until after he left St. Paul," Scott said. "At first it seemed like he called every day, and now it's about once a month. He and Charisse came to Dallas last winter to see a Cowboys game with my family, and he's treated my kids great, always remembering their graduations and birthdays with cards. It's been real neat the way things have worked out. He took the bull by the horns, all we did was provide him the stage."

As a Saint, Strawberry learned a lesson he reminds himself about to this day: "The main thing is that I saw if I kept battling, things would change. I also kept telling myself that I wasn't going to fall off the wagon."

Two years later, Strawberry is back on top.

"There aren't that many happy endings in baseball or in life," Goldklang says. "This seems to be developing into one."

May wasn't so hot. Strawberry's average slipped to .262 and he only hit two homers and drove in seven runs. But meanwhile he showed his teammates that he was in their corner by landing a crushing punch to the side of Armando Benitez's head during a May 19 brawl with the Orioles. And he was healthy.

But by the middle of July, Torre had a question about the left knee. He'd seen some things he didn't like. Even though

Strawberry had launched a 420-foot homer in Cleveland two nights earlier, the manager was thinking about putting him on the DL. Naturally, Strawberry fought it. One, he wasn't hurt. Two, he needed the at-bats to reach his incentives, and he needed to have a strong season so the Boss would pick up the $2 million option.

He was set to dig his heels in again. This time, instead of fighting addiction or a fractured image, it was the dreaded disabled list. He wouldn't call his bosses idiots or question their intelligence. But Strawberry knew his left knee wasn't a big enough problem to put him in dry dock. Sure, the knee wasn't as strong as he would have liked, but it had been good enough to bat .261 with 12 homers and 33 RBIs in 180 at-bats.

"Why me?" asked Strawberry. "All I know is that I'm fine and would love to continue to play."

Strawberry was concerned that with Bernie Williams returning from the DL soon, and Chili Davis slated back for the first week of August, the Yankees were looking to shelve him to make roster space. After a pre-batting practice talk with Torre, Strawberry admitted to feeling better about the situation. And GM Brian Cashman said then that Strawberry wouldn't be DL'ed for Williams.

"I don't anticipate shutting Straw down for Bernie," Cashman said. "But if it doesn't get better or look like it's not going to get better, then we'll have to take a look at it. If it continues to look bad, we have to do what's best over the long haul and what's best for Darryl."

With a 66–21 record and a fifteen-game bulge over the Red Sox in the A.L. East when they took on the Tigers at Tiger Stadium on July 15, the Yankees were quietly eyeing October. Torre and Cashman needed to know if Strawberry could help in left field, since they anticipated having the switch-hitting Davis to handle the DH duties.

"If we're fortunate enough to get to the postseason, you

don't want anyone on the twenty-five-man roster who can only hit and lumber," Cashman said. "That's not going to help Joe out."

During a five-game stretch from July 22 to July 29, Strawberry made a powerful point about his knee by hitting five homers and driving in eight runs.

"Best move I didn't make," Torre quipped.

August rolled around and Strawberry played sparingly. He eventually had his DH time reduced by Davis and didn't play much in the outfield. But there was something a whole lot bigger going on inside Strawberry's body and mind.

Nobody knew what it was, but Strawberry was different. Never real loud in the clubhouse, he wasn't a church mouse either. Now, however, he'd become withdrawn, and by the middle of September something was clearly bothering him.

By the end of the month, he was nursing a bruised left calf and Torre was talking about the possibility of not putting Strawberry on the playoff roster.

Strawberry proved he could run in the final weekend of the season by stealing a base and stretching a single into a double.

However, on Monday, September 28, he finally told the club about a searing pain on the left side of his stomach near his belt. He said it had been there for two months in the morning when he woke up. As the day progressed, the pain subsided. But now he wanted to get it checked. Strawberry had talked about it to Eric Davis, who was stricken with colon cancer in 1997, and Davis urged him to see a doctor.

Asked why he waited so long, Strawberry said, "I didn't want them to put me on the DL."

A blood test was followed by a CAT scan that revealed a growth. As the Yankees prepared for Game 2 against Texas, they were braced for the bad news that hit them the next day in Texas.

So, a season in which Strawberry hit 24 homers and drove

in 57 runs was over. As the Yankees got ready to sweep the Rangers, Strawberry was lying in Columbia Presbyterian Medical Center, scheduled for surgery to remove a malignant tumor from his colon. The operation would be a success, and the prognosis was good.

Even then, however, baseball wasn't entirely over. A man who had overcome so much had another hurdle to clear, perhaps the most important one in his life. But as he did with the booze and the drugs, this challenge would be met head on.

And this time, he had an entire city and baseball universe praying for him.

13

American League Championship Series: Tribal Warfare

Chided about their lack of offense during a three-game, pitching-propelled sweep of the Rangers in the A.L. Division Series, in Game 1 against the Tribe, the Yankees never let Jaret Wright, a cocky twenty-two-year-old right-hander breathe.

Consecutive singles by Knoblauch, Jeter, O'Neill, and Williams put the Yankees up 2–0 in the first. Wright wild-pitched another run and Jorge Posada booted Wright out of the game with an RBI single that made it 4–0. As Wright walked slowly and defiantly toward the third base dugout, the crowd of 57,138 let him have it. He may not have been throwing at Luis Sojo when he broke Sojo's wrist in spring training, but that's what the throng believed. Chad Ogea surfaced from the bullpen and was greeted by a run-producing single by Scott Brosius, for a 5–0 lead.

David Wells had more than he needed, clamping down on the Indians, allowing only two runs on five hits. Wells was now 2–0 in postseason play, allowing two runs in 16 1/3 innings and surrendering ten hits.

"To see Jaret go out in the first inning, I don't know how to say it [but it was] gratifying, all right," Wells said. "It was a good feeling for us because when you get five runs with the way we've been pitching, that's plenty."

"That was big," Joe Torre admitted. "It's the one thing if I was going to keep my fingers crossed, it was just let's get off the schneid pretty quick with Knoblauch and Jeter getting the base hits. This is what we've become used to seeing all year."

"The pressure is still on us," Paul O'Neill said prophetically. "As far as the series' momentum, [Game 2] is a huge game. We have to go out and swing the bats and hope [David Cone] has his good stuff."

Cone would deliver. But others wouldn't.

A championship heart that never missed a beat all summer faced its biggest test in Game 2 because Ted Hendry blew a call, Tino Martinez made a bad throw, Chuck Knoblauch ignored a live ball he believed was dead, and the Yankees turned into Men Without Bats again.

In the twelfth inning, with a 1–1 score and pinch-runner Enrique Wilson on first, Travis Fryman pushed a bunt toward Tino Martinez. Since Fryman was running on the grass inside the baseline, Martinez's throw hit him before he touched first base. Everybody in the Yankees universe believed Fryman was out. As the ball rolled toward right field, Knoblauch looked at Hendry and pointed toward Fryman, wanting an interference call that would return Wilson to first with one out.

"I was expecting the guy to be called out," said Knoblauch, who didn't hear Martinez and catcher Jorge

Posada yelling at him to get the ball. With the ball live and moving away from the infield, Knoblauch continued to point as Wilson toured the bases. By the time Knoblauch retrieved the ball, Wilson scored and Fryman made third.

Why didn't Knoblauch fetch the ball first and make his point with Hendry later?

"I didn't know where the ball was after it hit him," Knoblauch said. "Guys started to point around and then I picked it up."

Jeff Nelson struck out Brian Giles, hit Sandy Alomar, and walked Joey Cora. Graeme Lloyd surfaced and gave up a two-run single to Kenny Lofton that hiked the Indians lead to 4–1.

"When you play four hours and it's decided like that, it's a shame," said Knoblauch, who was 0–for–6. "But there is nothing you can do about it."

The Yankees could have done plenty about it a lot earlier than waiting around for the wild twelfth.

"It shouldn't have gotten to that point," said Martinez, who left Paul O'Neill at third base with one out in the fourth and the Yankees trailing 1–0. "I didn't do the job with the sacrifice fly and it cost us."

For the game, the Yankees were 1–for–11 (.091) with runners in scoring position. A team that batted .299 in the clutch during the regular season was hitting a disturbing .182 (8–for–44) in the postseason when it counted. Wasted by the dead wood and the bizarre play was a magnificent outing by David Cone, who went eight innings, allowed one run and five hits.

All everybody was dwelling on was the Play.

"I saw Knobby arguing and I kept going," said Wilson, who entered the game as a pinch-runner for Jim Thome. "I have to say that this is the first time I scored from first on a bunt."

"I got to the ball on the line and when I turned to throw it, I didn't see Knobby at all," Martinez said. "I don't think Knobby would stop and stare if he didn't think it was an out."

According to crew chief Jim Evans, who was in right field, Fryman's proximity to first base played a key part in Hendry not calling Fryman out.

"If a runner gets hit up the line with the ball and he's not in the [running lane] and it's what we determine to be a throw that had a chance to retire a runner, then he is out," Evans explained. "The play occurred right at the base. The fact that he was literally on the base or a half step off the base when it hit him, he has a right to be in that position."

Joe Torre wasn't buying that rap. Nor was he absolving Knoblauch for not going after the ball.

"They gave me some kind of reasoning, that he had to get back, in other words, he had to get out of those restraining lines to touch the base, which I agree with, except he was never within those restraining lines," Torre said. "He was on the grass, he was so blatant. I don't know what to say. It was a terrible call. Just for one guy to say what he saw and the other guy to swear by it and meanwhile you have it on video."

"I screwed up," Knoblauch would say later, after he viewed the replay. "I screwed up and feel terrible about that. I should have went and got the ball regardless of what the outcome of the umpire's call was."

And Yankee fans let him know it. At his next at-bat in

the bottom of the twelfth, he was greeted by a chorus of boos. It hurt him deeply, but he understood their disappointment.

"They were booing me for screwing up the play, and you can't fault them for that," Knoblauch said.

Before the series, it was assumed that the Indians needed a fluke to give them a game. Now, that fluke had happened. Now the heart that pounded so loud all summer needed to beat a little faster.

Suddenly, the Yankees weren't in the driver's seat. Not after losing a heartbreaking 4–1 decision in twelve innings to the scrappy Indians. With the best-of-seven series at 1–1, they weren't on life support, either. But for the first time since early April, they faced a huge hurdle in Game 3 at Jacobs Field.

Knoblauch's mental mistake in Game 2 opened up a lot of questions. Did the Indians have the Yankees number? Would the Yankees be able to jump-start their offense? Would Knoblauch's blunder live in infamy, ranking up there with Bill Buckner's miss of an easy grounder that lead to the Mets 1986 World Series victory?

Their fate looked promising at first. A leadoff single by Chuck Knoblauch and an RBI single from Bernie Williams gave the Yankees a 1–0 lead. Then Pettitte gave up a solo homer to Thome and an RBI single to No. 9 hitter Enrique Wilson in the second.

"The first two innings, I don't know if I was uptight or not, but I needed to relax," said Pettitte. "In the third and fourth I felt like I was settling down and thought I was going to pitch a good game."

Well, not exactly. When he retired Omar Vizquel and David Justice to start the fifth, Pettitte appeared to find a groove. And even when Ramirez drove an 0–1 pitch for an opposite-field homer to right for a 3–1 lead, no alarms went off. But a walk to Travis Fryman on a very close 3–2 pitch was followed by Thome's second homer, a towering drive to right that barely made it over the wall. Whiten, released by the Yankees last year, then hit a 3–1 laser to left to give the A.L. Central champs a 6–1 lead.

Thirteen pitches had produced three homers and forced Torre to lift Pettitte for Ramiro Mendoza.

The way Colon was dealing, it may as well have been 60–1, because the Yankees weren't coming back. Using both sides of the plate with a 95 mph fastball, and mixing in change-ups and cutters, Colon was the latest hurler to dominate the Yankees, who couldn't hit water if they fell out of a boat on nearby Lake Erie.

Suddenly, the Yankees were in a 2–1 ditch in the best-of-seven series, and were hoping Orlando "El Duque" Hernandez, who hadn't worked since September 25, could fill the role of a much-needed tow truck against what promised to be a sky-high Dwight Gooden.

A loss wouldn't end the Yankees record-breaking season, but the ditch would be deeper at 3–1 and put them on the verge of elimination.

"You are always concerned," David Cone admitted before the game. "We need to win [Game 4], we need a big night from El Duque and get our best pitcher [David Wells] on the mound [in Game 5]. We need to get it back to New York with a chance to clinch it. At least that's the way I'm looking at it."

Since El Duque hadn't pitched in fifteen days, the Yankees didn't know what they were going to get from the

Cuban refugee. They knew he had the heart and stomach to compete on the biggest stage of his life. Yet, the layoff was the X factor and it made for some uneasy hours preceding the game the Yankees had to have in order to avoid falling behind 3–1 in the best-of-seven series.

All the hand-wringing turned out to be for nothing. Hernandez delivered the goods, pitching seven shutout innings and allowing only three hits.

"To see something like that is neat," Paul O'Neill said of El Duque's performance. "This was the biggest game we played all year. We were playing for our lives out there tonight. He comes out and pitches out of trouble a couple of times and nothing affects him. He has been a big part of this team since he's been here."

Working in front of a lineup that couldn't break out of a postseason slump against Dwight Gooden, El Duque had to be as good as he was. The Yankees collected four hits and were batting a putrid .194 in the ALCS.

O'Neill homered off Gooden in the first and Chili Davis doubled in a run in the fourth. Tino Martinez, who stopped an 0–for–14 ALCS slide with a double in the ninth, plated a run with a sacrifice fly that Kenny Lofton dropped in the fourth. Scott Brosius's sac fly in the ninth provided the final run.

El Duque wasn't bothered by the sold-out ballpark or that the Yankees were, as O'Neill said, playing for their lives.

"I had pressure prior to the game. It was a big game and I knew we had pretty much a must-win situation. I had pressure, but I had no fear," El Duque said.

Needless to say, the Yankees walked out of the Jake feeling a whole lot better about themselves.

"We feel good, we are aligned well and have our best pitcher going [today]," David Cone said of David Wells. "One game can swing the momentum one way or another. I'm sure they feel good over there, but we have our best pitcher going."

El Duque had gotten them even in Game 4 with his seven shutout innings. Then came Wells, who had listened to tasteless remarks about his late mother, Ann, while he warmed up in the bullpen. To a man, the players had believed "Boomer" would point them toward the Bronx leading the best-of-seven series, 3–2.

"That's what got me out of focus," Wells said of the loudmouths near the bullpen. "I was [on the mound] fighting myself and I just said, 'I have a job to do.' I got out of it, 3–2, and I settled down after that."

Looking ahead, Wells wanted to lock up the series pronto. "You want to win it as quickly as you can. Anything can happen in [a Game 7] situation, and you don't want to be in that situation if you can avoid it. Cleveland is a bunch of streetfighters, it's scary. You could be the best team and get your butt kicked."

Thanks to Chad Ogea hitting two batters, walking two others, and Davis plating two with a one-out single in the first, the Yankees got the drop on the Tribe. Tim Raines's bases-loaded ground out presented Wells with a 3–0 lead before he threw his first pitch. Ogea's wildness would develop into a pattern for Indian chuckers, since they issued eleven walks and hit two batters.

However, the feeling of having presented one of their pitchers with an early lead vanished when Kenny Lofton lined a 3–1 pitch around the right-field foul pole and Omar Vizquel and Travis Fryman followed with singles.

Vizquel stole third and Fryman advanced to second on a wild pitch.

Manny Ramirez scored Vizquel with a fly to cut the lead to a run. Wells rebounded to fan Mark Whiten before walking Jim Thome. At 0–2 to rookie Richie Sexson, Wells caught him looking at a curveball, the pitch that would bail Wells out all day long and lead to his eleven strikeouts.

So, thanks to the gutsy pitching performance by Wells, a clutch relief job from Mariano Rivera, Chili Davis finally joining the band, and the inability of Indian pitchers to locate the strike zone, the Yankees took a colossal step toward reaching the World Series by posting a 5–3 victory over a wilting Tribe in Game 5 at the Jake.

Suddenly, the layers of anxiety that hovered above the best team in baseball two days ago had vanished.

"Now we have to get them in our hometown and beat the crap out of them," George Steinbrenner crowed in a clubhouse that was swollen with confidence but lacking an ounce of cockiness.

Derek Jeter had buried the Indians with a colossal two-run triple. Now, the hottest athlete in New York was looking to drown George Steinbrenner with a bottle of lukewarm champagne.

"Oh, Boss man," Jeter said as he spotted the Boss in the middle of an intoxicated Yankee clubhouse. "Oh, Boss man."

Then Jeter let loose a stream of champagne that soaked Steinbrenner to celebrate a 9–5 victory over the Indians that clinched the ALCS in front of a raucous Yankee Stadium crowd of 57,142.

Yes, the Yankees were back in the World Series, a baseball address they fully believe should always be their final October destination. Their ticket was punched.

Thanks to Scott Brosius, Ramiro Mendoza, and Jeter, the Bombers appeared in their 35th Fall Classic.

Brosius crushed a three-run homer in the third off Charles Nagy that extended the Yankees lead to 6–0. Then the huge and very vocal crowd watched the 6–0 lead dwindle to 6–5 in the fifth when Jim Thome reached the upper deck with a grand slam off David Cone, and things became tense. But Jeter's one-out, two-run triple to right in the sixth and Williams's single, which scored Jeter, upped the bulge to 9–5 and allowed the huge crowd to exhale.

"We still had a lead, they never tied it," Paul O'Neill said of the game being on the verge of a laugher and instantly turning into a white-knuckler.

Cone danced around danger in three of the first four innings but was scorched by Thome's grand slam in the fifth when the Indians first baseman punished a middle-of-the-plate slider. Still, Cone was the winner. In five innings he allowed five runs and seven hits. He was 2–0 in the postseason. Nagy absorbed a beating giving up six runs (three earned) and eight hits in three innings.

"I told them they picked me up," said Cone, who rebounded from Thome's bomb to retire Travis Fryman and Brian Giles on fly balls to left. "I let them back in the game. I was trying to get under [Thome's] hands and left it out over the plate."

As Thome watched the ball collide with a seat in the right field's upper deck, he believed the Tribe could come all the way back and force a deciding Game 7.

"For a minute, I thought that was going to get us over the hump," Thome said. "Then it turned around, but it's nothing to be ashamed about."

Mendoza worked the sixth, seventh, and eighth and didn't allow a run. Afterward, many pointed to his stint as the key to the game. Two defensive gems by Brosius also didn't hurt. Mariano Rivera recorded the final three outs to touch off a celebration on the field that was protected by an army of police.

They erased the Rangers in three games and dispensed the Indians in six. Now they were four wins away from adding the 24th World Series title to the collection. Only the dangerous and surprising San Diego Padres stood in their way.

14

The World Series: Catching History

After relying on their vaunted pitching staff to turn back the Rangers in the A.L. Division Series and the Indians in the ALCS, the Yankees had no reason to believe their dormant bats would wake up in the first two games of the World Series. It didn't mean they thought the Padres would win; it was that they had become so used to the pressure-packed world of close games dominated by their starters, middle relief, and closer Mariano Rivera that they expected more of the same. However, by the third inning of Game 2, the Yankees bat rack was alive and the number one reason the Padres were toast.

The first sign of life came in the second inning of Game 1 when rookie outfielder Ricky Ledee, making his first postseason start, doubled in two runs off Kevin Brown. David Wells gave up three homers—two to Greg Vaughn and one to Tony Gwynn. With a three-run bulge and Brown on the mound needing nine outs for victory, it appeared the Padres were going to get the drop on the Bombers.

Then the seventh inning unfolded. Chuck Knoblauch rocked reliever Donne Wall with a towering three-run homer to tie the score, 5–5. Tino Martinez, who went

5–for–30 (.167) in the first two rounds of the postseason and had listened to speculation that the Yankees would trade him to sign free agent Mo Vaughn, broke it open with a grand slam off Mark Langston.

"It was nice, I hadn't been doing much but we were winning and we were in the World Series," Martinez said. "I knew that I would come up in a situation where I could help the team win."

So, with a 9–6 win in Game 1 in the bag, the Yankees attacked Andy Ashby in Game 2 with three unearned runs in the first inning, three earned runs in the second, and another earned run in the third. Bernie Williams's first homer in the postseason came in the second and Jorge Posada clubbed a two-run bomb in the fifth.

Meanwhile, Orlando "El Duque" Hernandez confused the Padres with his various arm angles and tantalizing change-up. In seven innings, Hernandez allowed one run and six hits. El Duque was helped out by Paul O'Neill's leaping catch into the right-field wall on Wally Joyner's first-inning fly to right with two runners on base. Instead of having at least two runs off El Duque, the Padres were taking the field for what turned out to be a 9–3 whipping. Up 2–0, the Yankees jetted to San Diego.

But by the time Scott Brosius arrived at the plate in the seventh inning of Game 3, the tide seemed to be turning. The Yankees trailed 3–0, and if they lost, they were looking at Kevin Brown starting Game 4 for the Padres against Andy Pettitte, who would have had twelve days of rest since the Indians spanked him in Game 3 of the ALCS.

But Brosius's homer off Sterling Hitchcock gave the Yankees life. Shane Spencer followed with a double and scored on an error by third baseman Ken Caminiti. Walks to Paul O'Neill and Tino Martinez brought Brosius to the plate again in the eighth inning with the Yankees trailing 3–2. On a 2–2 fast ball from Trevor Hoffman, the best bullpen closer in the majors, Brosius homered to dead center field to put the Yankees up 5–3.

"This is the type of thing that you've dreamt about as a kid," Brosius said. "I've done this in my backyard a hundred times."

Mariano Rivera ended the game with runners on first and third by striking out Andy Sheets.

With a bottle of champagne in one hand and a World Championship smile, Derek Jeter finally admitted what many in the baseball world believed to be true.

"I don't see how you can say we aren't the greatest team ever," Jeter said in the aftermath of a 3–0 victory over the Padres in Game 4 of the World Series at Qualcomm Stadium, where the Yankees finished off an unbelievable season with a four-game sweep of the N.L. champs that delivered the second World Championship to the Bronx in three years. "We won 125 games and I don't see too many other teams with that. We are unselfish and we never care who the hero is."

In front of 65,427 juiced fans, the largest crowd to watch a baseball game in San Diego, the heroes came from odd neighborhoods.

Andy Pettitte, who hadn't pitched in a dozen days and had wrestled with his father Thomas's open-heart surgery the week before, provided brilliant pitching to atone for the beating the Indians laid on him in Game 3 of the ALCS. With Thomas Pettitte released from a Houston hospital the previous day, his son took the mound relaxed.

"I think it did help me," said Pettitte, who left the bases loaded in the second when Brown attempted to bunt his way on and was thrown out by Joe Girardi. "My father called me today and he was able to go home. That helped my mind be even more clear, that he was doing good."

Thanks to a stunning play by Jeter that turned a single to center by Ruben Rivera into an out, Pettitte retired nine straight from the end of the second to the fifth when Brown singled to right.

Bernie Williams staked Pettitte to a skinny 1–0 lead in the sixth when his chopper off the packed dirt in front of the plate was high enough that the only play Brown had was to first, and that was very close. Brown looked at Jeter racing home but decided he had no chance. His throw to first beat Williams by less than a half-step.

Jeter, who had two hits, opened the eighth with a walk on a 3–2 pitch. Paul O'Neill followed with a grounder to Jim Leyritz. Instead of tossing to Brown, who was covering the bag, Leyritz attempted to beat O'Neill to the base with a foot-first slide and didn't.

"I was safe," O'Neill said. "Believe it or not, these old legs got there."

Williams advanced the runners a base each with a chopper to Ken Caminiti at third. Tino Martinez was intentionally walked and Scott Brosius, the Series MVP, dropped a single into short left field that scored Jeter.

Ricky Ledee, who had a double and a single and four hits off Brown in the Series, got enough of a filthy sinker to loft it to left and score O'Neill.

"I had a 2–0 count and I was looking for a pitch to hit," Ledee said. "When he came with the sinker, I had to go with the pitch. I was a little in front of the pitch but got enough of it."

All that stood between the Yankees and their ordainment as the Greatest Team Ever were six outs. Mariano Rivera, who inherited a 2–0 count on Caminiti from Jeff Nelson and gave up a single, left the bases loaded by getting Leyritz on a liner to center to end the eighth. Rivera worked around a couple of hits but induced Carlos Hernandez to hit into a 6–4–3 double play that negated Rivera's cousin, Ruben, who started the ninth with a single to right.

Bernie Williams, who more than likely was playing his last game in pinstripes, drove in a run with an infield out, and Series MVP Brosius plated a run with a bloop single to left in the two-run eighth.

When Rivera induced pinch-hitter Mark Sweeney to hit a routine ground ball to Brosius, Rivera tracked Brosius's throw across the diamond. When it settled into Tino Martinez's leather, Rivera dropped to his knees and raised his arms toward the night. Finally, the lone goal for any Yankee team owned by George Steinbrenner had been reached. What they had sweated for under a blazing Tampa sun in February was now reality.

"I was thanking God for everything," said Rivera, who had three Series saves and six in the postseason. "I threw [Sweeney] a cutter for the double play. I knew he was an inside hitter and I went with the cutter anyway."

It was the Yankees 24th World Series title, the most championships won by a single franchise in any sport.

"When you talk about going 125–50, that's a phenomenal year," said Paul O'Neill. "I don't care how we got it done, we got it done. All year long it's been somebody else's week. This week it was Scott Brosius's week. And the way Andy Pettitte pitched, it was meant to be. To win four in a row and sweep the World Series puts an exclamation point on it. This is a special season. What we accomplished won't be done for quite a while."

From there it was showers of champagne.

Acknowledgments

Thanks to my wife, Debbie, for understanding the bizarre life of a baseball writer and putting up with the BS associated with it.

In 1993, I was involved in a book project with Bill Brown, the best baseball writer who ever lived. The subject was the Phillies, a team we covered for separate newspapers. The Phillies had to win the World Series for our work to be published. So when Joe Carter took Mitch Williams deep in Game 6 to lift the Blue Jays to a World Series title, the project crash-landed. Less than two years later, Bill Brown went off the air after cancer tapped him out. Now it's a different league in a different city, but it's still sportswriting and he was the best. Thanks, Bill. My round.

To Greg Gallo and Dick Klayman, thanks for the chance to be part of the *Post*, the best sports section in America. Thanks to Hondo's gang of night owls. Ditto to Howard Ball, Rich Wallace, Scott Hayes, Brian Malone, and Jim Gauger for other chances given.

Thanks to Mauro DiPreta, Anja Schmidt, Toisan Craigg, Elliott Beard, April Benavides, Tracy Heydweiller, and Susan Weinberg at HarperCollins.

Get well, Straw.

About the Author

Prior to becoming the Yankees beat writer for the *New York Post* in January of 1997, George King worked for the *Trenton Times* covering the Phillies from 1989 to 1996 and served as a New York sports bureau for the *Times* from 1986 to 1989. He has also worked for the *Greeneville (Tennessee) Sun*, *Boonton Times Bulletin*, *Suburban Trends*, *Daily Advance*, and *Meriden Record-Journal*.

George and Debbie King reside in northern New Jersey when they aren't in Anguilla or Martha's Vineyard.